HAMMONDS of HULL

‘A Store of Good Things for Family and Home’

John Markham

Highgate of Beverley

Highgate Publications (Beverley) Limited
2004

British Library Cataloguing in Publication Data.
A catalogue record for this book is available from the British Library.

ISBN 1 902645 39 1

Published by

Highgate of Beverley

Highgate Publications (Beverley) Limited
4 Newbegin, Beverley, HU17 8EG. Telephone (01482) 886017

Printed by Highgate Print Limited
4 Newbegin, Beverley, HU17 8EG. Telephone (01482) 886017

Contents

Page

Hammonds!

Of all the places God hath made,
Or human feet have ever strayed,
I speak the truth, I'm not afraid,
It's Hammonds.

It's not a place you like or lurk,
Your duties there you cannot shirk,
In fact you really have to work,
At Hammonds.

The Management are very kind,
A better lot you'll never find,
Except when G. G. comes to mind,
At Hammonds.

Staff training at Hammonds is all very well,
Taught as we are by Mr. Thirkell,
I wonder how many of us wish him in —!!
At Hammonds.

And when I leave this earth below,
And to my Maker I do go,
I will ask Him, "Did You ever know –
HAMMONDS"

Preface

Hammonds has always had a special place in my affection. From childhood, when I lived in Hedon, it was always an essential part of any visit to Hull. I was delighted, therefore, when an article on Hammonds I wrote for the *Hull Daily Mail* resulted in a letter from Christopher Powell inviting me to his home to see his collection of historic material on the store which had been run by his family for so many years. I was even more delighted to be offered the use of this archive to enable me to write a history of the store. While working on this project I have had considerable help from Christopher on many aspects of the text: I express my gratitude to him and other members of the Powell family who have been so supportive. For information on more recent years, since the take-over by House of Fraser, I am indebted to Geoff Kingston, Store Manager in Hull.

So many people have spoken, written or telephoned me with their memories of Hammonds and offering the loan of material that I feel certain I shall fail to acknowledge all those who have helped in their different ways. For information specifically used in the text I am grateful to: Mick Cook, Martin Craven, Audrey Dunn, Alec Gill, Roger Gill, Kitty Harker, Peter Heelas, William Jackson, Juanita Lewington, Neta Lowe, Audrey Lynch, Val Marsden, Joan Marshall, Mary Mawer, Stuart Moore, Geoffrey Ovington, Marjorie Perry, John Sanderson, Lilian Shearsmith, Tony Westoby and Bob Wrightson. For errors or omissions I apologise in advance. The comments of many, though not individually recorded, have been invaluable in helping me to acquire a full picture of the store and the people who worked there. Once again I acknowledge the excellent proof-reading services of Ian and Margaret Sumner.

One problem I cannot claim to have satisfactorily solved. In its early days Hammond's was always given its grammatical apostrophe and the name of the limited company formed in 1913 was always Hammond's. Yet, no doubt under the influence of new styles of advertising, the apostrophe disappeared from general use in the 1950s. My compromise solution, to use Hammond's until the opening of the new store in 1952 and Hammonds thereafter, is not totally correct by any criteria but it is, I hope, an acceptable way of resolving this dilemma.

October 2004 John Markham

Foreword

By Christopher S. Powell

I calculated that during the 1960s Hammonds employed about 5% of the population of Hull in some way or another, whether it be on a fulltime basis, or just for Saturday, or Christmas jobs. Most of these people tell me that they have happy memories of their time in the store. Yes, there had to be rules, but the ethos was for people to enjoy their jobs. I like to think the fact that they did enjoy themselves is why customers enjoyed the shopping experience at Hammonds.

Personally, the twelve years I spent in the store fulfilling various roles were happy ones and I particularly enjoyed being involved in the training and development of some of the staff. There were four of the fourth generation and we were all cousins. All had their role to play: Bill looked after the properties, Tim bought china and glass, then became director of the Bridlington store, Mark was the fashion director and I, having been involved with staff training and buying for various departments, became director of the household departments, as well as giving around 250 talks about the history and policy of Hammonds to various groups throughout the region. When I married I was already booked for so many evenings that I had to ask my secretary to limit the number to one a month and she was heard to say, 'He's out so often, the wife and the dog both bark at him.'

There is no doubt that the success of the store over that period was due largely to the team my father, John Powell, had gathered together after the war and especially the triumvirate of himself and the two Geoffs. Geoff Knight was an accountant who liked the i's dotted and the t's crossed. Geoff Wilson was the creative driving force behind the buying and selling. Despite the fact that they both had the same ultimate aim, their methods of achieving it differed, and so it was my father's role to smooth the path to success.

Funny incidents come back to me, such as two entries in the monthly report that the nursing sister used to send to my father: 'Wricked neck when trying on swimming costume', and 'came over all unnecessary when caught shop lifting'.

On the first day of the sale we took a double full-page spread in the *Hull Daily Mail,* and – as account customers enjoyed a preview of sale merchandise, some lines would run out before the first day, so there had to be last-minute alterations to the advert. These could get rather complicated and mistakes occurred. For example, under the heading Ladies Underwear and Kayser Bondor Shop, the list read: Ladies' cotton briefs reduced to 1s. 11d.; ladies' nylon slips reduced to 2s. 11d.; galvanised dustbins complete with rubber lids etc. (corsetry with a vengeance!).

John mentions the incident of the firework on the top floor. The fire practices we had had over the years proved successful but there is nothing like the real thing to find the problems. Strict instructions were issued not to use the word fire, as it could create panic. Despite there being billowing smoke on the other side of the glass dividing wall, some customers, when asked to vacate the Picadish, said to the increasingly nervous fire officer for that floor, 'Thank you, lad. We'll just finish our fish and chips and we'll be with you!'

I think that people particularly liked the fact that it was one of the family who came to give their group a talk on the history of Hammonds and indeed there were many times when I learnt a lot from the post-talk reminiscences of group members. However, they were the source of a lot of amusement. The third talk I gave was to the aptly named Gas Women's Federation: 'Go to the gas showroom and listen. You'll hear where we meet.' I was still rather nervous about giving talks and this was exacerbated when I was greeted by the secretary with, 'Don't worry, I'll try and keep them quiet.' I was once embarrassed when I sneaked in at the back of a hall so as not to disturb the 'business of the meeting'. I was spotted by the chair lady who, with a look of relief, cut a member short when she was enjoying her 'moment of glory', describing her visit to the annual meeting of the WI at the Albert Hall. 'Thank you, Mrs. —. Excellent. Mr. Powell has just arrived.' And initiated a round of applause.

On another occasion, the stove hadn't been lit in the scout hut where the WI met so the chair lady, a large lady in a coat that had taken a flock of sheep to make, announced 'We will wear our coats and Mr. Powell will give a *short* talk.'

It is over 30 years since I left Hammonds and yet there are occasions when I am still greeted as 'Mr. Christopher' and enjoy a reminisce with a former employee. More interestingly, members of the public like to reminisce about what they flatteringly call the heyday of Hammonds. I felt that if there was still so much interest in the store and its role in the life of Hull, a record should be made of its history. I had done some research into the history, so that I could give talks to various groups, in my role as public relations officer, and had gathered together papers and photographs relating to the various events that had occurred in the store over the years, some of which had been handed down from previous generations. I handed these to John Markham hoping that they might help him to write a history. He has added so much more to the story by very diligent research. He has related the growth of a business to the growth of Hull and the prosperity of the country as a whole, which makes this book so much more fascinating. I thank him for doing justice to a subject that has been such an important part of my life as well as the lives of those who worked in and shopped at 'The Store' throughout the generations.

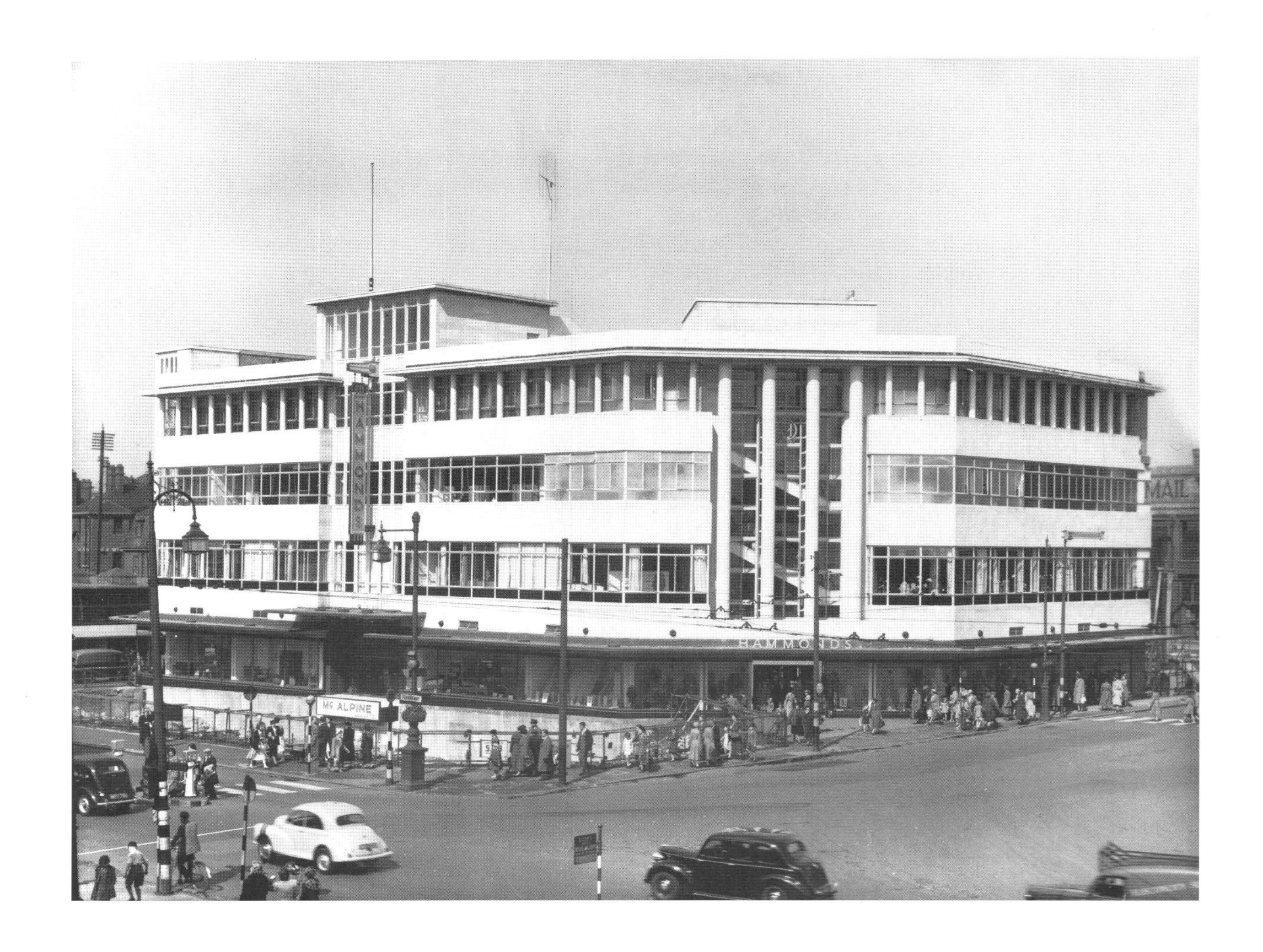
HAMMONDS
HAMMONDS
Mc ALPINE
MAIL

1

H. W. Hammond: North Bridge and Osborne Street

It was a day of destiny when two of James Powell's three sons, William and Henry, travelled from Brighouse to Hull in 1889. The purpose of their journey was to value the linen and drapery business in Osborne Street, founded by H. W. Hammond at an earlier location and still trading under his name, though he had died in 1874 and it was then owned by a Mr. Wells.

James Powell, the founding father.

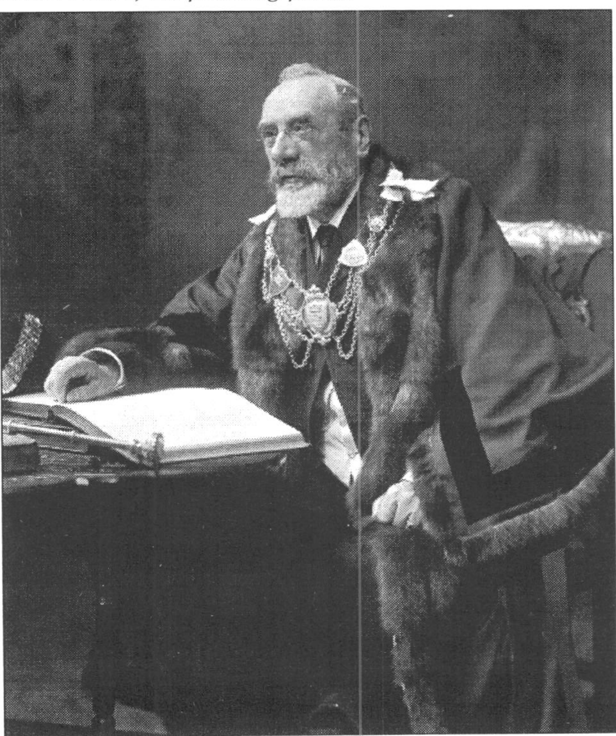

An oral tradition that the business passed to a man who had followed a much-trodden route to fortune by marrying the boss's daughter is, unfortunately, apocryphal. Hammond died a bachelor and (apart from bequests to his 'faithful housekeeper') appointed his 'friend and foreman' Richard Johnson trustee for the rest of his possessions, which were to be divided between two nieces and a nephew. By the time the Powells travelled over to make their valuation it was a large and flourishing concern, well established in Hull and beyond as a shop offering wide choice and giving good value.

James Powell, the father of the trio, was a man of considerable commercial experience who had trained in London and Paris. For 30 years he had been based in Brighouse and Wakefield combining his drapery business with his professional practice as a valuer. An illustration of the Brighouse shop reproduced on an invoice shows crinolined ladies and top-hatted gentlemen outside an elegant emporium of classical design, with an impressive entrance surmounted by a pediment bearing the single word, Powell. The windows appear to be attractively dressed. A two-storey building rises behind the single-storey frontage. James Powell is described in the invoice heading as Silk Mercer, Linen Draper and Haberdasher, his merchandise consisting of Shawls, Mantles, Bonnets, Flowers, etc., etc.

Obviously attracted by the potential of Hammond's, the Powell sons not only valued the business but went further and bought it – according to family tradition without waiting for their father's consent. James, was a shy man, but he also displayed considerable courage in relying on his two sons' judgement, moving home and setting up in business in a new town when he was already so well-established in the West Riding.

Hammond's became a name synonymous with Hull, famous throughout Yorkshire and well outside its boundaries. Yet the man whose name the store bears is

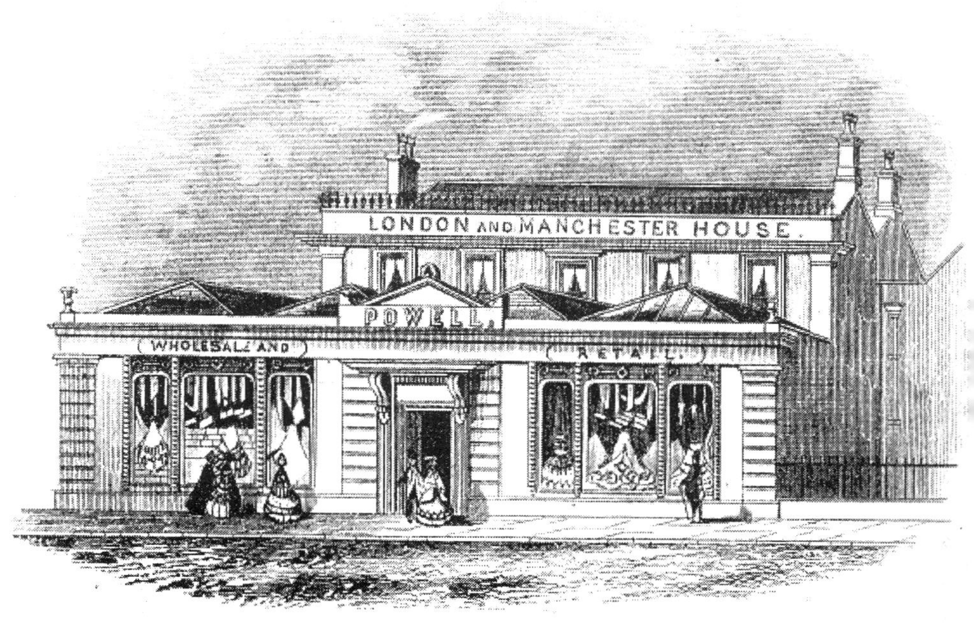

James Powell's shop in Brighouse.

a shadowy figure. For nearly a century. 1821 has been celebrated as the year in which the business was founded but the evidence is far from certain. The earliest mention of that date so far discovered by the present writer comes in a document of 1913.

Early directories contain a number of Hammond entries, at least one of whom appears to be a relation, most probably H. W. Hammond's father. In 1791 Henry Hammond was listed as merchant and W. Hammond Esq. as shipowner, but it is George Hammond, cornfactor of North Street, who holds most interest. By 1826 George's home was 7 Myton Place, the address at which both he and H. W. Hammond, draper and hosier, were living in 1831, the first directory reference to the embryonic entrepreneur and to his first shop at 4 North Bridge. He next appears in the 1838 directory (these were published irregularly) and by 1840 he had acquired additional premises, at 27 Wincolmlee. By that time his address was given as 7 Castle Row. A similar entry appeared in 1842. A little more information comes from the 1841 census, the first to list individual names. There he was described simply as Henry Hammond, linen draper, born outside Yorkshire (a later census gives his birth place more specifically as Brigg, Lincolnshire) and living with two Hammond relations, both Yorkshire-born and of independent means: Elizabeth aged 74 and Mary, 40, quite probably his mother and sister. Surprising, though, is his age, 36, which would make him only 16 in 1821, the year in which he reputedly started his business near North Bridge: not an impossibility for a young man from a family with a certain amount of money, but neither is it likely. A foundation date a few years after 1821 seems more realistic. This caution over uncritical acceptance of the claimed opening in 1821 is given some support from a publication of 1891 stating that the history of the firm extended back 'over a period of about sixty years'. The problem is, however, complicated by an advertisement of 1819 discovered by an earlier researcher which states that one of the outlets for Warren's Paste (a boot and shoe polish) was Hammond's, North Bridge, Hull. Hammond would then have been only 14 or 15. A possible solution is that he eventually took over from an older relation previously in business there.

His previous connection with Hull is unknown. Even if it were nil, he had made a wise choice opening his business there, selling cloth for making clothing at home, and house furnishing material such as serviceable calico, serge and red flannel. The opening

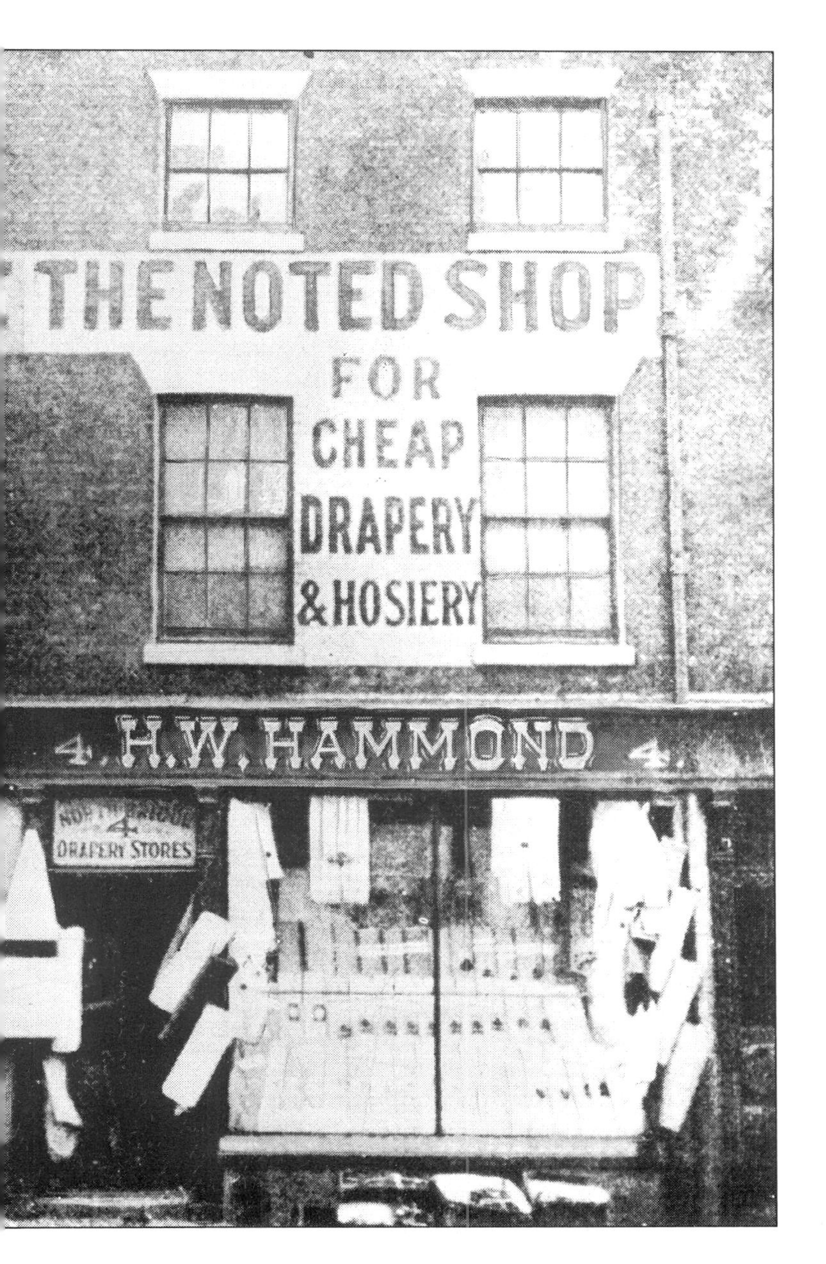

of the first dock (later named Queen's Dock) in 1778, followed by Humber Dock in 1809 and Junction (later Prince's) Dock in 1829, had added enormously to Hull's trading potential. The population was growing; so too was wealth, and a shop near North Bridge was convenient for the residents of such smart addresses as George Street, Charlotte Street and other streets of tall town houses in Hull's Georgian suburbs as well as for people of lesser means living at addresses which did not quite carry the same cachet.

In 1846 and 1848 Hammond was still in business at North Bridge and in Wincolmlee but his home address was further west, in Osborne Street, first at No 17 later at No 31, an augury of future development. His lifestyle seems somewhat peripatetic and in a period when renting was more common than ownership he had moved to 10 Silvester Street in 1851. Ten years later the census shows him again living at 31 Osborne Street, now described as a 56-year-old bachelor lodger of Mary Hammond the putative spinster sister, who derived her income from railway dividends.

A momentous change came in the 1860s when he decided to locate his business in Osborne Street, almost certainly because he realised Hull's centre of gravity was moving in a westerly direction away from the Old Town. In particular, it was much handier for Paragon Station than North Bridge. The station's main entrance was in Anlaby Road, only three minutes from Osborne Street, an important advantage as the railway brought potential customers into Hull from considerable distances.

At first Hammond occupied one shop, No 31 Osborne Street, later expanding into the building

H. W. Hammond's shop at North Bridge.

next door. His business flourished in its new location and, when he died in 1874, after suffering from general paralysis for three months, his home address was 66 Park Street, a fashionable part of the town. His estate was valued at under £8,000, a not inconsiderable sum.

Expansion continued after his death. In 1879 a new shop was erected on a site formerly occupied by two dwelling-houses, 35 and 37 Osborne Street and also Hick's Court, one of Hull's many yards tightly packed with cottages behind the main streets. These improvements made it the largest shop in the area. By the time the Powells appeared on the scene, it stretched impressively from No 31 to No 41.

It was certainly visually striking. Four storeys high, it was entered through a lobby paved with Minton tiles, and with doors of American walnut. On either side were handsome windows 12 feet wide, a startling contrast to the small-paned windows to which most were accustomed. Inside, the emphasis was on another novel concept, undivided space. From the large open ground floor a fine staircase led to another open showroom, wood-panelled on ceilings and walls like the one below. Above the public areas were two spacious workrooms, a kitchen and dining-room, and on the top floor storage space and other rooms. Some would be the quarters for employees who lived-in, like H. G. Wells' Kipps.

Hull's best-known ironmongers, King & Co, had installed a central heating system of hot-water pipes and another sign of technical progress was a new system of gas lighting, the albo-carbon, which gave 'a remarkably clear and almost white light of great power and brilliancy', the first time it had been used in any shop outside London. Attached to the new development were two other shops, one for carpets and one for heavy drapery goods. The whole premises covered nearly 700 square yards.

Unfortunately, according to the *Eastern Morning News,* Osborne Street itself was unequal to this grand edifice. Its paving – in this context, its surface – was disgraceful and there was an urgent need to cut a long-talked-about street connecting it with Carr Lane. Ultimately Hammond's had to move in order to achieve its full potential.

Printed rules to be obeyed by employees were based on both moral and commercial principles. All derived from an unequivocal opening statement:

1. We require that every individual be attentive, polite, and persevering to the rich and poor alike, and never to lose sight of the fact that the poor person who can only spend one shilling, and gives this establishment the preference, is as much entitled to attention as the most affluent.

Strict procedures were laid down to govern every aspect of business:

2. Every article is marked in Plain Figures, the selling prices, from which no deviation can be made. But in all cases where there is difficulty in serving a customer, whether the price or the article be the obstacle, no customer can be allowed to leave unserved without the question being first referred to the shop-walker or manager.
3. All parcels of goods to be delivered must have the name, number, and address written legibly thereon in ink, with number of Assistant who sold the goods, also the amount to pay on delivery, if anything. All parcels sold during the day must be in the parcel room before leaving at night.
4. Any Assistant sending out goods and omitting to get them entered, or receiving back and omitting to get them made returned, which must be done by fetching the clerk from the office in both cases [*sic*]; also, the shop-walker to call back the goods in both cases. All goods entered must have a bill, written in ink, enclosed. No entry to be made of goods without calling the shop-walker.

5. Each article must be clearly specified for dissection [*sic*] and the writing and figures unmistakably plain and clear. Each Assistant will be held responsible for every check in his or her book, and, should any be missing, must be signed for by the shop-walker or the manager before checking in the book, or be fined 6d.
6. No assistant can be allowed to promise the delivery of any parcel at any hour, other than those appointed, until he has ascertained whether it can be sent.
7. Each assistant is requested to be scrupulously careful in counting the cash received from their customers. Also the change received from the cashier. Any assistant taking counterfeit coin shall be fined 6d. and make good the amount.
8. All applications for goods to exchange or return must be referred to the shop-walker or manager.
9. All salaries will be paid the second Friday in each month. No entries of goods will be made to any assistant, and any assistant buying goods in the shop must buy them on Friday before noon and at no other time. The goods will be charged the regular price, less 10 per cent where the profit will allow it. The discount must be taken off and all goods called back and the check signed by the shop-walker or manager. No assistant will be allowed to bring a parcel on the premises or take one off the premises. Anyone breaking these rules will be instantly dismissed.
10. The first party to be in the shop at 8 a.m. prompt, the second party at 8.30 a.m., and no-one will be allowed to go into the house after that time. No assistant will be allowed to leave the shop during business hours without the permission of the manager.

Penalties were prescribed for every conceivable departure from this code of conduct – some surely only to be expected in a busy store and likely to be pardoned in a later, more tolerant, age:

11. For forging a number.
    For each article left out of parcel.
    For omitting own number on bill.
    For signing an incorrect bill (and forfeit amount in error).
    For not signing a bill (if examiner).
    For signing a bill without properly calling the goods back.
    For not presenting bill at desk with cash.
    For not adding up book and putting in a total paper before leaving at night.
    For an indistinct bill.
    For promising to send a parcel at either delivery and neglecting to do so.
    For an incorrect address.
    Any assistant shall be fined 6d.
12. Talking, laughing, or congregating together in departments – fined 6d.
13. Any assistant being ill must at once have the doctor sent for, and any assistant being ill or not at business on Monday morning will be fined three days' pay unless the doctor certifies that they are unfit for business.

Even in non-working hours staff were subject to a highly disciplined routine:

14. Breakfast to be on table at 7.30 a.m. during the week, when all must be down; the table to be cleared at 8.30 a.m. prompt. No smoking allowed in any part of the house except the front sitting room, and on Sundays not until dinner is cleared away. All lights to be out and doors locked at 11 o'clock prompt. Anyone coming into the house intoxicated or using obscene language will be instantly dismissed.
15. All assistants are expected to go to St. John's Church (where seats are provided) at least once each Sunday, or regularly attend some other place of worship.

2

James Powell & Sons

The Powell brothers must have quickly assessed the potential of the business. It had a good pedigree, it was prosperous, it was managed by owners who were alert to new ideas and who had demonstrated that expansion was profitable, and it was in a town already with a proven record and with an optimistic future. Hull provided them with a far bigger stage for exercising their commercial talents and implementing ambitious plans then ever Brighouse could do.

An advertisement in the Hull press on 8 October 1889 announced the purchase of H. W. Hammond's business and James Powell & Sons' intention to carry on under its familiar name, news which would be a relief to conservatives, who preferred continuity to change. It also indicates that the name was already synonymous with a reputation which the new owners were keen to maintain. In order, however, to re-establish it as they wished, the Powells were holding a grand clearance sale of the whole stock, which they had bought at a very large discount on the cost price. Extraordinary bargains were offered, the shop remaining open until 7 pm, the sale fortunately continuing through Hull Fair week when many out-of-town visitors could be expected.

The Powell father and sons (the third son, Samuel, an engineer, joined the firm in 1895) brought renewed vigour and a keen business acumen to the already successful store, making substantial alterations and improvements, buying adjacent houses and adding a uniform frontage to the various buildings, now extending 178 feet, and with an impressive façade which ultimately reached from No 27 to No 45. Experience and contacts made in the West Riding were brought to Hull. As outstanding specialists in all types of wool they were to attract customers nationally and internationally. A contemporary directory was no doubt justified in claiming that the display in the large and lofty plate-glass windows was a constant source of interest and attraction to passers-by and that the Osborne Street emporium was to be compared with 'one of the great drapery and furnishing depots of the west end of London'.

The growth of Hammond's coincided with the growing prosperity of Hull. New docks on the side of the Humber made it one of Britain's leading ports, fine public buildings symbolised its self-confidence and pride and in 1897 it received the royal accolade of city status. A book published that year, *Men of the Period – In England – The Record of a Great Country,* includes a eulogistic account of Hammond's, eight years after its purchase by the Powells:

'Nos. 31 and 33, Osborne Street accommodate the boot and shoe department, with separate fitting-rooms for ladies and gentlemen, and the tailoring department, with a fine stock of piece goods for "bespoke" work of the best class, as well as a large assortment of ready-made clothing, stylishly cut and well finished. Next door (No. 35) the firm sells small-wares and sewing machines, doing a large trade therein; and after this we reach the main entrance to the emporium, comprised in the handsome and spacious double-fronted shops, Nos. 37 and 39, Osborne Street. Here all manner of ladies' fashionable requirements are to the fore, including everything new, choice, and tasteful in dress fabrics, silks, velveteens, corsets, laces, gloves, ribbons, trimmings, furs, fancies, and untrimmed millinery. The Manchester department, [goods which came via Manchester from the Lancashire cotton mills] admirably accommodated at No. 41, makes a fine show of goods peculiar to it, embracing prints, linens, calicoes, shirtings, sheetings, etc., and there is also a well-chosen stock of men's mercery, rugs, bags, umbrellas, and other articles of outfitting. The firm's general offices are above,

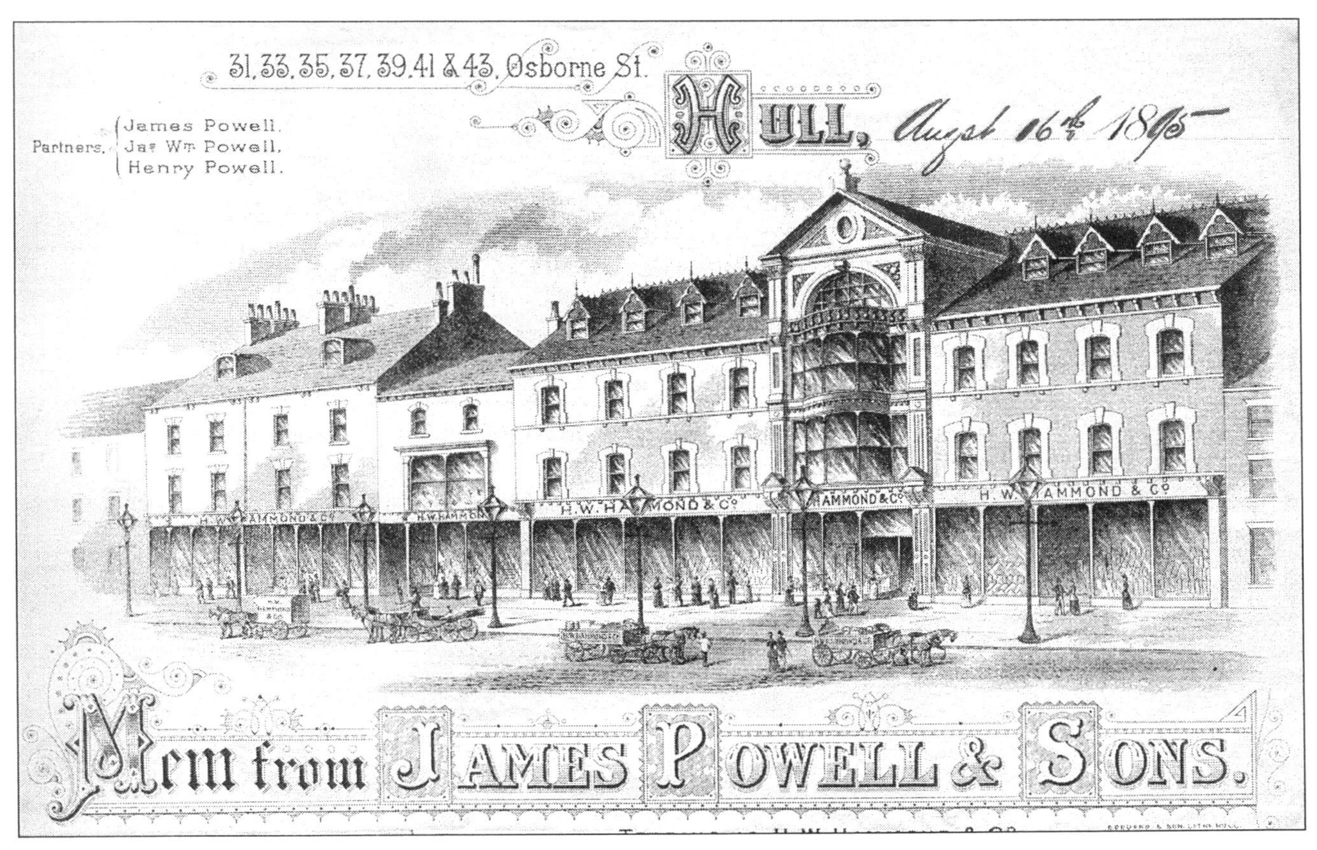

H. W. Hammond's premises in Osborne Street.

together with other departments incidental to the commercial routine. The shop numbered 43 and 45, Osborne Street, is an exceptionally large one, 120 feet deep by 35 feet wide, and here Messrs. Hammond display one of the most complete stocks of furnishing goods to be found in Yorkshire. Everything required for the equipment of any kind or style of house is *en evidence* in the greatest variety, and the show of furniture in the great salons on the first and second floors it would indeed be difficult to surpass. Over the various shops the first floors intercommunicate, and the visitor passing through them makes further acquaintance with the firm's enterprise through the medium of the elegant and attractive showrooms devoted to millinery, mantles, shawls, ladies' underclothing, and baby-linen. The latest London and Paris fashions are exemplified, and excellent accommodation is provided for ladies in the way of private fitting-rooms. The firm has a special

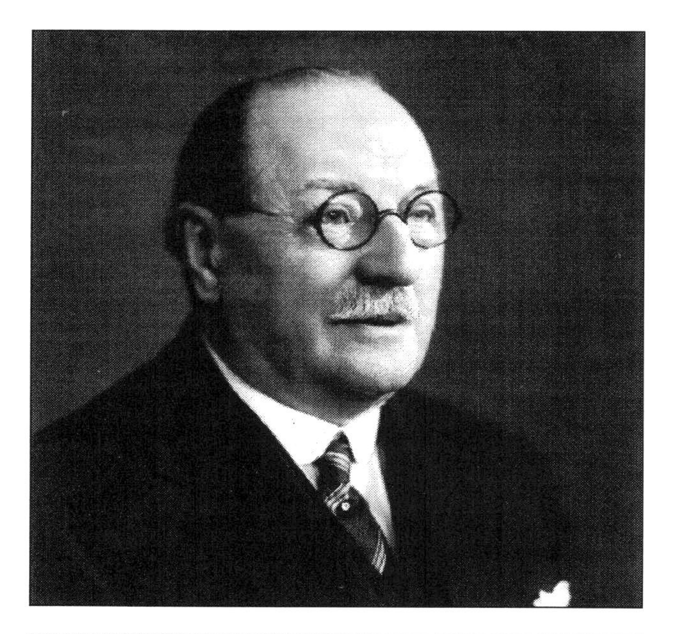

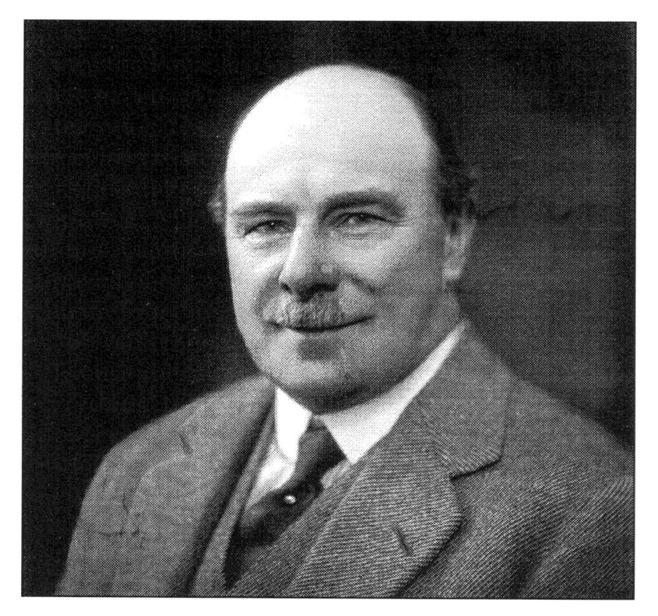

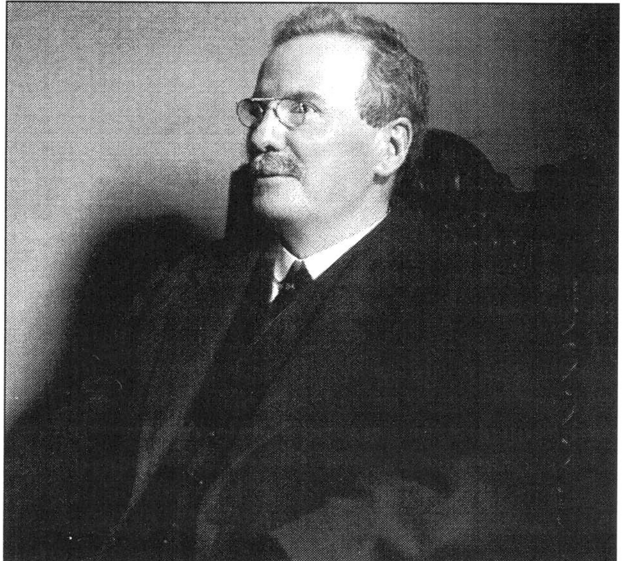

The sons of James Powell:
(James) William, top left.
Henry, bottom left.
Samuel, top right.

room for receiving commercial travellers, and another special department is the parcel *despatch-room,* always presenting a busy scene. Admirable arrangements exist for the rapid and regular delivery of goods by means of the firm's own vans; *and mention must* be made of the system of sending out patterns, etc., by post, whereby large numbers of customers can avail themselves of the advantages of the establishment without the necessity of a personal visit. The latter, however, is the only means by which it is possible to gain any idea of the immense provision made by Messrs. Hammond to meet every requirement of the public in such matters as pertain to the drapery, outfitting, and furnishing trade. The firm's connection extends throughout Hull and for miles around, and their vast business necessitates the employment of many assistants, whose comfort and general well-being are carefully considered. Everything supplied by Messrs. Hammond is a speciality in the sense that it is first-class value for money, and one of the best examples of this is found in their "Defiance Navy Serges", a splendid range of fabrics, greatly and deservedly esteemed.

'In conclusion, we must mention the large valuation business carried on by Messrs. James Powell & Sons. This is a most important branch of enterprise, and embraces all work connected with valuations, arbitrations, transfers, sales of business, stocks, etc., in the drapery, outfitting, and furnishing trades. Messrs. Powell are known all over the United Kingdom in this connection, and their extensive knowledge, sound judgement, and ample experience combine to bring their services into great request.'

The age of the walk-round store was still to come but no one entering Hammond's could be unaware that this was a prestigious business which regarded the supply of its goods and services as a matter of some gravity. A frock-coated gentleman, known as a shop walker, would greet customers at the door, find out what they required and obtain a salesman to look after them, a system which continued in some shops into the 1930s. Customers were not free to walk round and inspect goods by themselves. The salesman's modest weekly wage was supplemented by commission and, regrettably, in spite of all the stern rules, they gave short shrift to those assessed as having little money to spend.

Chairs were placed before counters so that customers could be free of physical strain as they made their difficult choices, courtesy was taken for granted with everyone addressed as sir or madam, parcels were expertly tied (an assistant in another Hull shop was dismissed in the 20th century for a badly tied knot) and doors were opened for effortless entries and exits.

Hammond's advertising, far more formal and wordy than it later became, shows an eagerness to please which at times touches on the obsequious. One advertisement of 1907 reads: 'We pay particular attention to coloured wools and silk threads and carry such an immense stock that, even if you do not start the work in hand from our stock, we can match you the right colour and quality you have been using with the right material. It is no trouble to help you in the sometimes difficult task of matching wools or silks.' In another advertisement they emphasised the availability of their world-wide mail order service for wool: 'Responsible supervision is given to all post orders, but, if you feel you are not receiving the attention to which you are entitled, a note addressed to Mr. Powell would be appreciated.'

Invoices surviving from the Osborne Street days are beautifully headed with an engraving of the fine façade, outside which smart people stroll and hansom cabs patiently wait, along with a smaller picture of the North Bridge shop, a reminder of the humble birthplace of this flourishing enterprise. Handwritten details of the goods purchased include the amount handed in and the identifying numbers of the employees who served the customer and examined the document, the transaction being ratified by the application of the Hammond's stamp – the apostrophe which eventually succumbed to the wishes of advertisers and marketers still inserted in an age which valued grammar and correct punctuation.

By popular request the shops now stocked New Art Blinds: 'The numerous enquiries which have been made for an Artistic Blind which will not fade have caused us to introduce the above which we guarantee will not fade in sunshine or washing, and further undertake to replace every blind which fails to fulfil this statement Free of Charge.' For ladies anxious to avoid the 'objectionable sympathy' of friends for looking too old, Hammond's supplied the perfect solution: 'Our

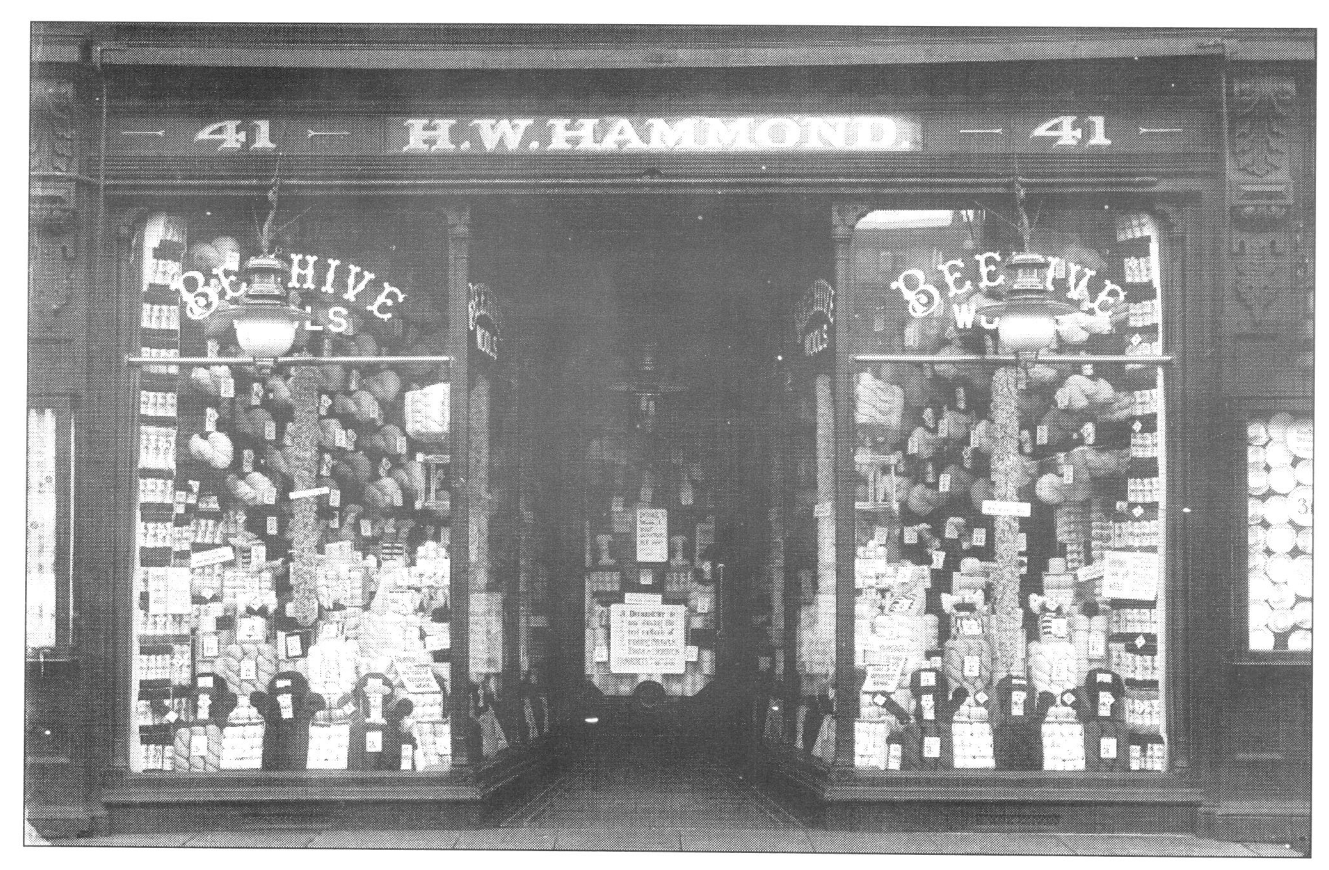

Osborne Street windows.

Corset Department aims at contributing all the advantages obtained by stocking the leading makes and the most fashionable shapes in such a variety that the individuality of every client is preserved and maintained.' Both the cottage and the mansion, it was claimed, could be tastefully and expeditiously equipped with all their needs, and, for the privileged few who had a telephone, one could have direct communication with every department.

John Powell, grandson of James the founder, and himself a future Chairman of Hammond's, had boyhood memories of some of the Osborne Street staff: Miss Dales, who looked after the showroom and ladies' fashions; Miss Large, buyer of millinery, who also operated a side-line in the form of an intimate café consisting of three marble-top tables and a gas stove behind a screen, where she provided the most important customers with a cup of tea; Mr Todd, buyer of furs and

An early replacement of horse-drawn vehicles.

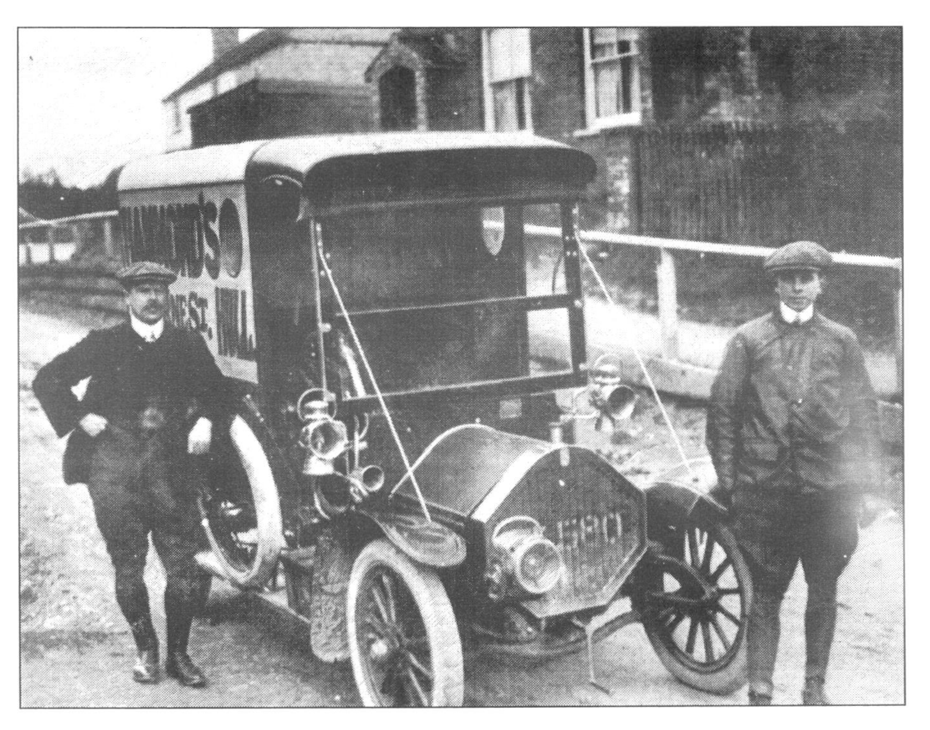

jewellery; Mr Teddy Hartell of Display; Mr McDonald, who walked the floors, looked after customers and made a magnificent sight with his white beard and frock coat; Mr Leek, another floor walker, who radiated such authority that he was sometimes mistaken for James Powell senior himself; Sergeant (he did not merit a title), head commissionaire and ex-policeman, who kept the shop front and the pavement spotlessly clean and received tips from customers who arrived in their carriages; Mr Frank M. Jones, buyer of wools, haberdashery and household merchandise, who was later to become General Manager of the store in Paragon Square; and Jim Bootyman, whose role is not recorded but who served Hammond's as a highly esteemed employee for 64 years. A later improvement, supplementing Miss Large's private café, was a Refreshment Saloon where 'ladies can now regale themselves during the fatigue of shopping with a cup of tea or other light refreshment.'

Very much in evidence were the three Powell sons. The eldest was (James) William (born 1861, who acted as father and adviser to the whole family, the second, Henry (born 1865), for a time buyer for all three Manchester departments and Samuel (born 1871) who bought furniture, bedding, ironmongery and china. Family businesses are prone to problems rising from the close relationships of their executives. The Powells, however, appear to have worked well together with no evidence of internal conflict. They were different personalities, each with his own area of specialisation and expertise.

What struck young John Powell most, perhaps unsurprisingly, was not the shop front and the goods on sale but 'the horses and splendid stables, the beautifully polished harness and the horse-drawn delivery vans', all of which created a powerful visual image of the superiority of a firm where customers could have their purchases conveyed to them in such grand style. Three horses and vans were constantly on the go, delivering twice daily in all parts of Hull.

An immaculate front-of-house needed an efficient organisation behind the scenes. To the rear of the main building were well-equipped workshops for cabinet-making, joinery and polishing. Nos 37 and 39 Osborne Street contained dining rooms and dormitories for over 40 living-in assistants, whose regular closing time of 7 pm was extended to 10 pm on Fridays and midnight on Saturdays and who accepted discipline, conditions and rules which seem unbelievably onerous to later generations.

There were boarding-school rules requiring prompt attendance at meals served at stated times according to one's place on a rota, and it was forbidden to linger in the domestic quarters when one's presence was obligatory in the shop. One anecdote from Hammond's early history is that the housekeeper served rice pudding daily until a daring deputation asked for a little variety. Apparently she responded by serving sago ever after. On James Powell's birthday, however, there was always a celebratory treat: plum pudding. Another story from the Osborne Street era is that tea and toast were served to staff at 10 am, a surprisingly lenient interlude in a tight regime. A photograph survives of two of the last employees who lived 'above the shop'. Though intolerably controlled and restrictive by modern standards, these working conditions were considered not only acceptable but far-sighted in their day. 'Almost the entire staff,' wrote one approving commentator, 'dine in the establishment daily. Messrs Powell are to be congratulated upon the excellent arrangements they have made to promote the personal comfort and social welfare of their numerous employees, who are certainly fortunate in being in the service of a firm so thoroughly considerate of their various wants.'

The last of the living-in staff: Teddy Hartell – left;Mr. Fletcher – top right with pipe.

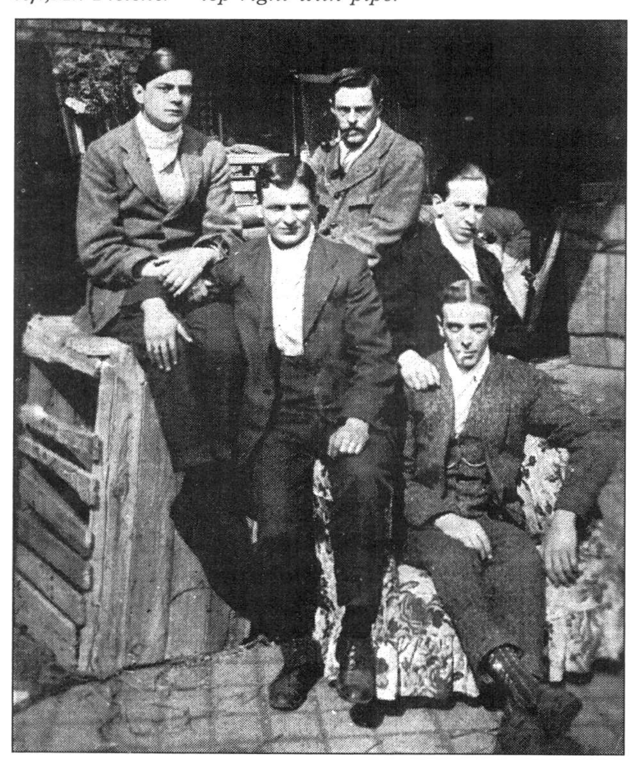

In an indenture whose formidable wording was enough to terrify a young girl, Edith Hodgson undertook to be bound apprentice in 1893 to H. W. Hammond in upholstery and carpet making. For the first six months she received no wages, for the next six months 2s. 6d. per week, and 3s. 6d. in the final year. Along with Edith, (James) William Powell and Henry Powell signed the document and her father, John Henry Hodgson, made his mark. All must have gone well as two years later William Powell certified that Edith had complied with the terms of the contract.

The strict routine was disturbed by a breakdown of electricity which affected business in central Hull on the evening of 12 January 1903. It could hardly have come at a worse time. There were claimed to be 2,000 customers in the shop when the lights failed as 350 assistants coped with the exceptional rush on the first day of the January sales. Whether Hammond's struggled with candles or, like some other shops, closed down early is unrecorded.

When Hammond's had a major celebration in 1971, graced by Royalty, a number of elderly people were proud to draw attention to their memories of Osborne Street. Mrs Edith Brown of Wyton Bar, who could boast of being a Hammond's customer for 60 years, wrote to John Powell: 'When I was a child of 7 years I remember riding to Hammond's in Osborne Street on a tram with my mother to buy corsets, French kid gloves, black botany wool stockings and needlework by the card for our undies. Then as I got older, coats, muffs and furs came on approval to our home as mother had bought a business and could not leave it. My Saturday night out was to go to Hammond's and pay the bills, we were always cash customers, and get perhaps, myself a blouse or pair of gloves.'

A Hedon woman recalled being taken as a small girl by her grandmother to Osborne Street and buying a silver teapot, and one who had been a pupil-teacher would visit the shop for material for the girls' needlework lessons: 'I remember vividly that the floors were uneven and creaked somewhat.' More recently, a near centenarian has happily reminisced about falling in love with a doll in the store. It cost 2s. 6d. and she named it Wendy after the character in *Peter Pan*.

A disciplined environment had the advantage of developing a corporate spirit and it was one that the Powells encouraged by organising group activities. Some of the events were ambitious. In 1901, for example, staff travelled to the Dukeries of Nottingham for their annual picnic. There was a perfect opportunity for a party in 1904 when James was elected Sheriff of Hull, an office which gave its holder a prominent role in public life

Garden party at Beechwood, Driffield, 1905, during James Powell's year as Sheriff of Hull.

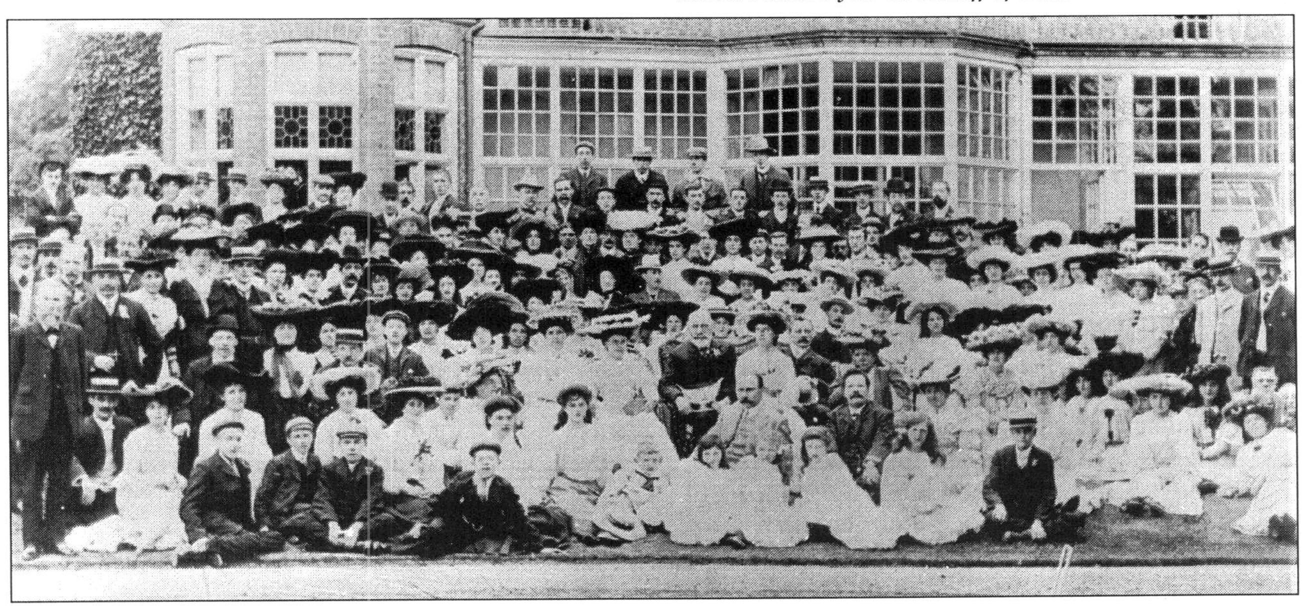

(which his shyness made him very reluctant to accept) and proof of the status which Hammond's had achieved in the eyes of the community and of civic leaders. After the Sheriff's chain had been placed round his neck James Powell 'stated that no one was more surprised than himself when the office was offered to him. He was always of a retiring disposition and consequently felt great diffidence in accepting the office.'

Invitations were issued to the staff to attend a garden party at Beechwood, the Driffield residence of The Worshipful The Sheriff of Hull. At 2.30 pm on Thursday, 20 July 1905 (by then a half-day holiday), employees left Paragon Station by special train and on arrival at Driffield about 3.15 pm proceeded to Beechwood, where they were 'shewn' over the grounds.

Sports – a 100-yards handicap race for men, 50 yards for ladies, an obstacle race and a potato race – took place from 4 pm to 5 pm when tea was served. An hour later, and surely unwisely in view of the amount which would be consumed, sports resumed. An egg and spoon race for ladies was followed by a men's tug of war (married v single) and, finally, a ladies' skipping race. At one point, not shown on the programme, there must have been speech-making and prize presentation, any taint of professionalism prohibited by the printed rule: 'No person shall take more than one prize'.

At 8.25 pm the train departed for Hull, though not before the obligatory photograph of the assembled party in front of the balconied façade of Beechwood. Over 250 faced the photographernd, whether he had failed to ask for smiles or everyone was overpowered by the historic importance of the event, the result was a mass of solemn faces. Occupying the place of honour, seated in an elaborate basket chair, was the paterfamilias, James Powell, white-bearded, his lapel bearing a bloom from the garden of Beechwood, holding a filigree silver fruit bowl (still in the family's possession) presented to him by his proud employees to commemorate his year in office as Sheriff. His moustached sons and their ladies were nearby. With rare exceptions, the men wore hats – boaters, bowlers or caps. All were in suits with collars and ties and, as far as one can see, waistcoats, with a number of watchchains in evidence: not really the gear for sports. Apart from a few children (members of the Powell family?) all the ladies wore large-brimmed hats, a fashion which resulted in smaller employees to the rear of the group being for ever excluded from this record of a happy and memorable day.

Even if Hammond's never achieved a royal warrant, they received a significant mark of recognition when Hull City Council commissioned them to arrange the décor and furnishing of private apartments at the Assembly Rooms (now the New Theatre) which were to be placed at the disposal of the Prince and Princess of Wales (the future George V and Queen Mary) on an official visit to Hull on 12 May 1903. The *Hull Times* enthused: 'The Princess and party's room is a perfect picture. The walls are draped with pleated blue and white cloth, with a red, white, and blue fresco valance. An artistic drawing-room suite, of the Louis XVI pattern, is set out on an Axminster blue carpet, with a border containing several colours. The windows are draped with curtains, and before the eventful day banks of flowers from the outside will be raised several feet above the ledges. Toilet rooms are also specially provided and elaborately fitted for the Princess and the twenty ladies or so who will accompany her. The Prince's room is treated in similar fashion. The suite has been upholstered in specially selected material, and from the windows the Royal party will look over banks of flowers at the scene in the street.'

Three years after the garden party at Beechwood James Powell died on 24 July 1908. The full panoply of mourning traditional in that period was accentuated by his prominence in the community and the respect in which he was held. As well as family mourners and staff, there were representatives of many business houses in Hull, and freemasons present included two from the Brighouse Lodge of which James Powell was the only surviving founder member. The plain oak coffin was brought by train from Driffield to Hull, where a number of employees who had been with the firm from 15 to 30 years, along with James' coachman and gardener, acted as pall-bearers. The staff tribute was a wreath depicting a broken harp. It was, in an obvious sense, the end of a chapter but there was no break in continuity. The triumvirate of brothers had worked closely with him and their managerial policy was well established.

3

Paragon Square

Though Edward VII had died in 1910, the sunshine of the long Edwardian summer did not fade until 1914. In 1911 there were two major social events. The annual picnic was to Matlock, with a train leaving Cannon Street station (the Hull and Barnsley terminus) at 6.50 am with breakfast on arrival at the New Bank Hotel. After a day's indulgence in the pleasures of Matlock, dinner was served at the same hotel before the journey

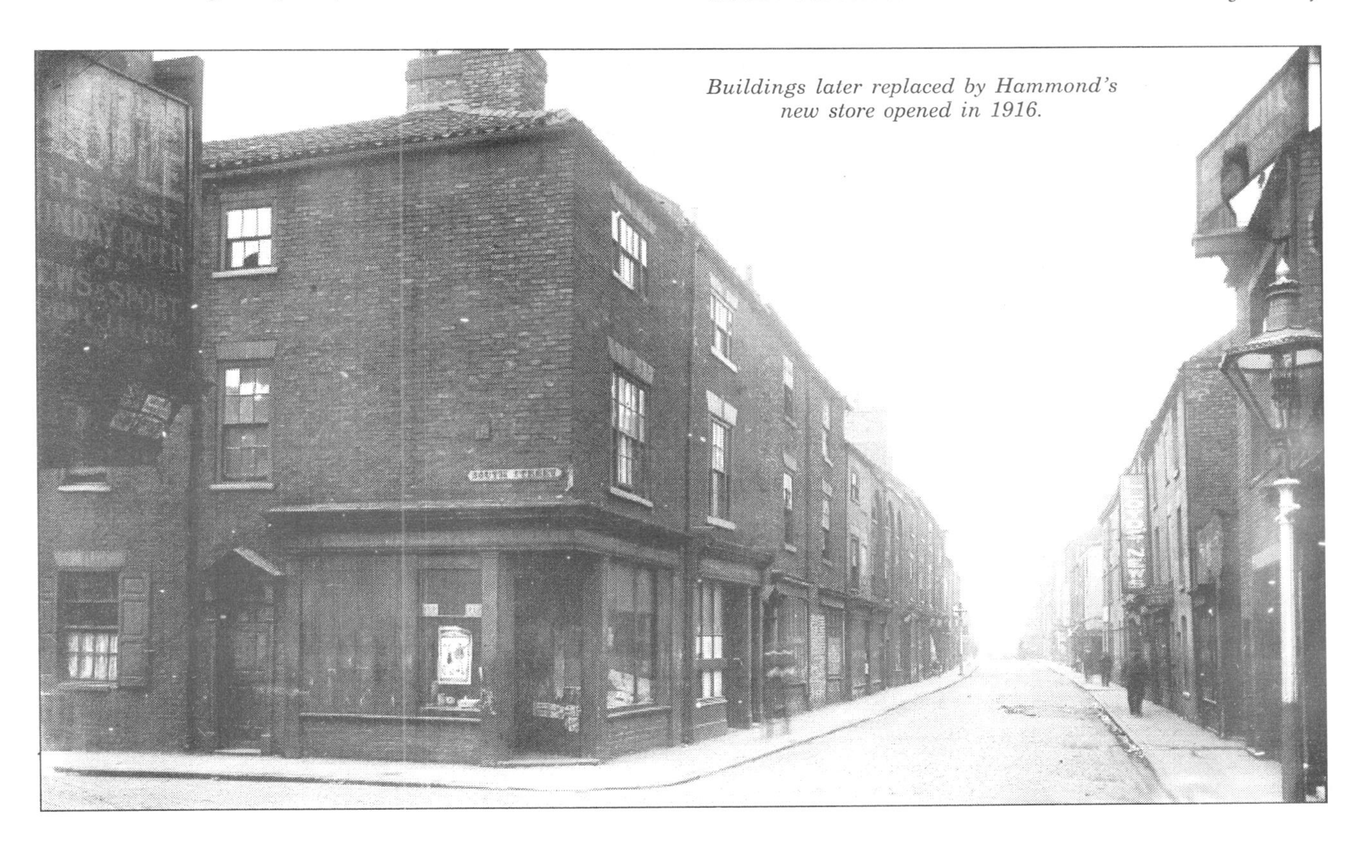

Buildings later replaced by Hammond's new store opened in 1916.

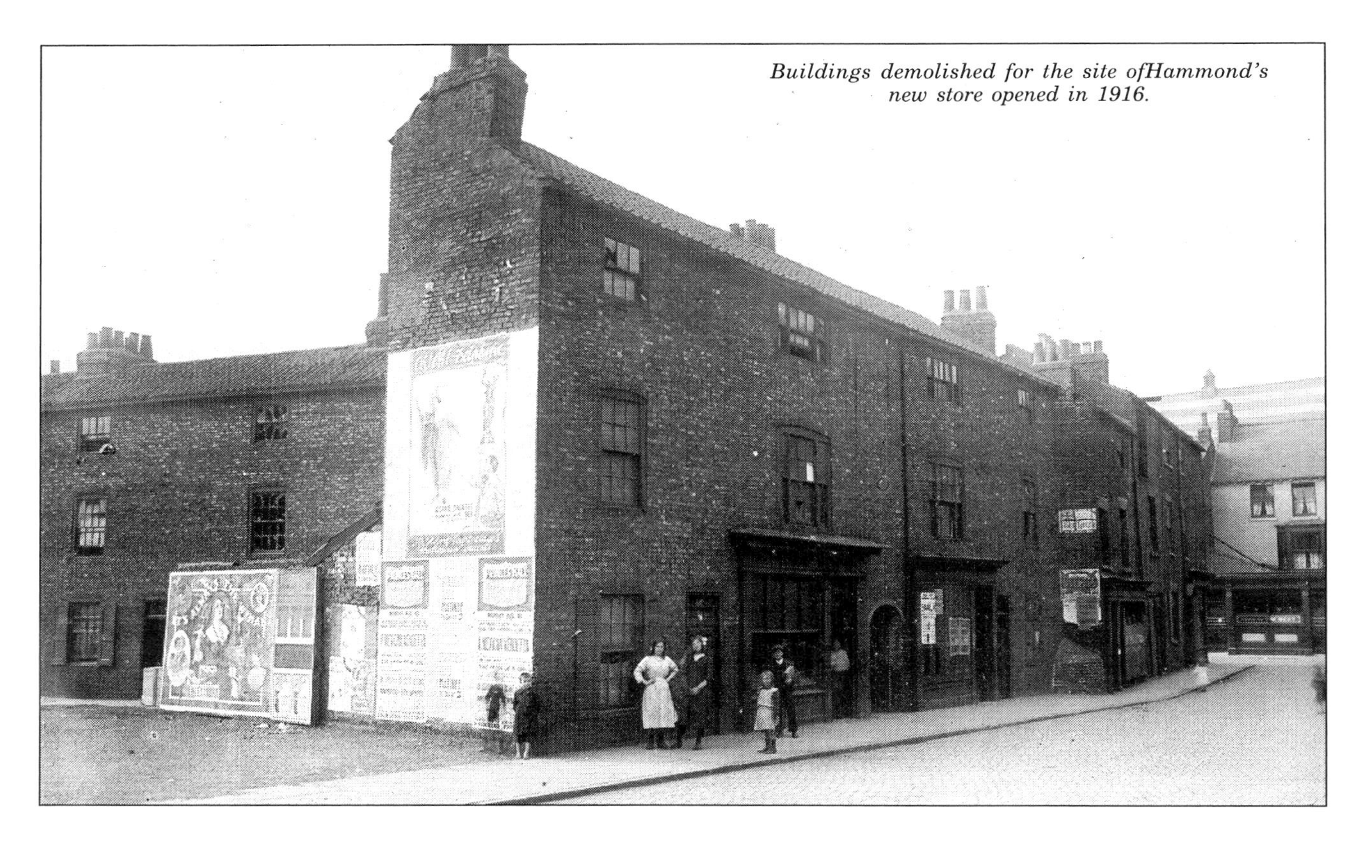
Buildings demolished for the site ofHammond's new store opened in 1916.

back to Hull by 9.55 pm, all for 8s. 6d. (42½p) – and for a prompt start the next morning after a rare full-day's closure of the shop. Three weeks later Mr and Mrs Samuel Powell hosted a garden party at their home at Tilworth Grange, Sutton. On this occasion waggonettes took employees from Osborne Street for entertainment which included tea in a marquee and dancing on the lawn until the waggonettes returned to Hull at 9 o'clock. Three photographs were taken: of the whole group and of men and women separately. The men wore boaters and the women in the front row adopted a Pre-Raphaelite pose, but there was no hint of frivolity.

It seemed an unchanging world but it was soon to be ended by war. For Hammond's, too, a momentous event in their history was on the horizon, and one which even war was not allowed to interrupt. Although the Osborne Street premises had been given a new façade and converted as far as possible into the accommodation needed by a flourishing business, the buildings were old and the basement damp. In a low-lying area not far from the Humber, flooding was frequent and pumps had to be in continuous operation to keep it clear of water.

In addition, the centre of Hull was evolving in a direction which left Osborne Street out on a limb in an area of poor public transport. Paragon Station had been 'turned round' so that its frontage no longer faced Anlaby Road but Brook Street: before the cutting through of Ferensway it stretched further south than it does today. In 1907 Jameson Street had been opened, creating a wide and impressive route from the station to Prospect Street and the new King Edward Street. For Hammond's there was a serious consequence: the new layout directed shoppers, especially those arriving by train, away from Osborne Street.

By 1912 the three brothers had started a serious search for land on which to build a new store. They lighted on an island site which had a superb location, substantially the same as that of the present store, bounded by Brook Street, West Street, South Street and Jameson Street, consisting of approximately 4,615 square yards of freehold land, nearly an acre in extent. By coincidence, some of the land for the new store was purchased from John Wilson, a tin canister manufacturer and, like the Powells, attracted from the West Riding by Hull's commercial potential. Samuel Powell, third son of James senior, married John Wilson's daughter, Mary, and all their children took the second Christian name, Wilson. John Wilson decided to build a factory next to one of his two best customers, Reckitt's, later selling out to them. Years later John Wilson Powell, son of Samuel, told a Hull audience that, if fate had so decreed, he might have been speaking as Chairman of Reckitt's rather than of Hammond's.

As well as the purchase of a plot of 628 square yards on the north side of Jameson Street, the project involved contracts with the owners of a large number of shops in Brook Street, South Street and West Street. Old photographs show the rows of decaying late Georgian properties which had to be demolished. One elderly Hull resident, Kitty Harker, who contributed her memories of childhood to a collection of similar pieces, entitled *Young Fogeys* and edited by Audrey Dunne and Alec Gill, recalled the scene: 'I can remember some very tall houses in West Street, before Hammond's was built. They were five storeys high. Some were lodging houses, used largely by immigrants who used to sneak in rent-free. I remember visiting these premises as a child. The houses smelt dirty and the inhabitants had dirty feet and clothes. I had to hold my nose when I went in.'

So far Hammond's had been a partnership. Now, with the need for more finance, a private company was formed, Hammond's Limited, with an issued capital of 60,000 Ordinary Shares of £1 each and 60,000 Cumulative Preference Shares of £1. The object of the share flotation, it was explained, was 'to provide the necessary capital for the purchase of the land and the erection of a new and up-to-date store'. The valuation business, 'one of the oldest established and most important of its kind in the provinces', was to continue as James Powell & Sons, but it was to be incorporated in the new limited company and would contribute to its profits.

The three brothers, William, of Woodside, Hessle, Henry, of Park Avenue, Hull, and Samuel, of Tilworth Grange, Sutton, would be permanent managing directors of the company during their lives. Both William, the Chairman, and Henry were described as drapers and valuers, but Samuel as draper only. They had fixed their total remuneration at £1,800 a year (i.e. £600 each), a modest salary, as a consequence of their ownership of all the Ordinary Shares and their confidence in being able to rely for the major part of their income on the profits which the new premises would generate. Investors were impressed by Hammond's track record and its prospects. Most of the Preference Shares offered were taken up locally, and many years later more than half the issued capital was still held by people living locally or having local associations. Yet there were those who, with inborn northern pessimism, forecast failure. The outbreak of war while the project was in its infancy and the trauma of Zeppelin raids on Hull must have increased support for their tidings of woe which, fortunately, events proved unfounded.

In Osborne Street business continued as normally as it could. World war was not allowed to prevent Hammond's maintaining its reputation as the leading supplier of wool by issuing a comprehensive guide to rug making, crocheting and knitting, accompanied by a price list of the materials needed for following the patterns. The illustrations are a delight, pictures from a lost world. A Boy Scout's knitted jersey (modelled by a nervously smiling boy in knee breeches and long stockings), a crochet cover for a hot water bottle, a handy tea cosy, ladies' winter sports gaiters ('To reach to the knee'), child's first drawers in crochet-tricot, and, rather daringly, 'Hug-Me-Tight' ('A useful jacket in crochet for wearing under a coat'). There was, though, the warning, to be repeated at the beginning of the Second World War, that goods were in short supply and no guarantee could be given that prices would not be increased.

The architects for the new store were the well-known Hull firm of Gelder and Kitchen, though a later Chairman specifically attributed the design to one of the partners, Llewellyn Kitchen. This is almost certainly correct. Such information would be known within the Powell family: Alfred Gelder was so prominent in Hull City Council affairs (later being knighted for his civic role and becoming an M.P.) that his personal involvement in some of the designs credited to the partnership must have been minimal; and Kitchen is generally agreed by experts to have been a far better architect than Gelder and more likely to have designed a building of such quality. The issue of the plans under the name of the partnership would not necessarily be proof of joint work.

The new store was intended to be an architectural adornment to the city. Location, size and design all contributed to its grandeur. The frontage on Jameson Street was nearly 100 yards long, that on Brook Street, facing the station, almost 60 yards, and Paragon Square was now 'one of the principal centres of the city'. The building's merits could be described concisely in professional language: 'A modern adaptation of the classical style of architecture was favoured for the store, with a central dome and pediment, a balcony surrounding the flat roof, and rusticated corners which carry a fourth tier of windows above the cornice to give proportion and added dignity to the building.' The *Hull Daily Mail* went further in extolling its virtues. 'The main décor,' it enthused, 'appears to be a wide-spread colonnade of massive stone columns supporting a deeply enriched entablature, the whole surmounted by an open balustrade rising to a height of over 50 feet above the footpath.' The dome, 25 feet in diameter and rising to a height of 90 feet from the footpath, would be a landmark in Hull, which was now becoming a city of domes. The triple-domed Dock Office, the City Hall and now Hammond's gave Hull a distinctive sky line.

It also gave Hull a new concept in marketing. No longer a mere shop, it was what the *Hull Daily Mail,* adopting terminology decades before it became common, described as a super-store, one of the first in the North of England. Shopping would no longer be a simple commercial activity which merely involved walking to a counter, being served with the goods you required, paying and then leaving. Now it was to be a social occasion, a positive pleasure. 'Anyone,' an encouraging advertisement announced, 'is at liberty to walk through the entire establishment and make an inspection of our immense stocks in all departments without being pressed to purchase.'

The idea of a store consisting of a multitude of departments selling (as the entrepreneur William

Whitely reputedly said) everything from pins to elephants, originated in 19th-century Paris with the establishment of Bon Marché. This innovation was adopted first in the United States and then in Germany, but, according to architectural historian Nicolaus Pevsner in his *History of Building Types* (1976), British department stores began later, in the 1900s. Harrods had begun as a grocery store in 1849 but the present building dates only from 1901-5; perhaps significantly it is in the French Renaissance style. Whitely also started in a small way in 1863, but built a new-style department store in 1908-12. Selfridges similarly dates from 1908. Outside London, Lewis's opened a department store in Liverpool in 1912-18, later in Birmingham, 1926-29, and Leeds, 1929-32.

The Powells, therefore, were in the forefront of progress when they purchased land for their store in 1912. Hull people of that period did not regard themselves as living in an isolated, backward area. In retailing Hull was one of the two pioneers of the North and not far behind London. To lure customers into their palatial emporium incorporating all the latest designs and ideas 7,000 square feet of glass attracted passers-by to stop and gaze at window displays backed by light oak panelling on a scale quite beyond those shown in contemporary photographs of shopkeepers standing proprietorially beside windows packed, inartistically, with their wares. There were three entrances, the main one in Jameson Street, another at its eastern corner, entered from South Street, and a third opposite Paragon Station, perfectly placed for rail passengers to walk straight in. The interior, it was justifiably claimed, had been planned with the utmost ingenuity and originality. Everything was on view in an open-plan system which provided ample space for avenues which led customers seductively from one department to another.

An anonymous newspaper reporter waxed lyrical about the delights to be savoured: 'On entering the premises from the Paragon Station is the department set out with art serges, tapestries and curtains. The whole length of the front windows from the station entrance to the main entrance in Jameson Street are devoted to the heavy drapery goods. The internal fittings of the different departments throughout are in light oak, and they are artistically designed specially to suit the class of goods, and with the idea of keeping it well in view, in the best condition, free from dust and yet easy of access.

'In another department a display is made of flannels; in another of prints, voiles, and delaines [light woollen dress-fabric]; in another, electric plate; in another, soaps and perfumery like a chemist's shop; in another, art needlework and silk embroidery. Others are for general haberdashery, trimmings, laces and veilings, ribbons and needlework, neck wear and handkerchiefs, hosiery and gloves, stationery, fancy and leather goods, dress selection, gentlemen's mercery, and outfitting. Along the whole length of each corridor the oak cases with glass fronts are pleasing to the eye, and, indeed, all the internal arrangements are in a quiet and dignified style.'

On the ground floor alone, 500 feet of counters allowed shoppers to make their purchases in comfort without delay. Discreetly located at the South Street end of the ground floor ('situated so as to enable customers shopping in this section without their seeming to be still in the drapery and fancy section of the establishment') was the gentlemen's bespoke tailoring department. Near this sedate enclave was a suite of offices for buyers, typewriting and housing the telephone. A young lady looked after 35 extensions and four trunk lines, with direct communication with the Corporation exchange and links to all departments. From this operational centre James Powell & Sons also conducted their valuation and fire loss business. Following the new fashion in London stores, the basement was no longer regarded as a no-man's land for storage and assorted behind-the-scenes activities not for the eyes of the public but, for the first time in Hull, a well lit, well ventilated shopping area.

A prominent feature of the interior was a grand staircase leading to the first-floor showroom. It was 12 feet wide, constructed entirely of oak, handsome marble columns adding to its dignity and helping to transform shopping from a routine transaction into an aesthetic experience. The showrooms were described as the finest in the North of England. From the millinery department customers moved through a display of blouses into ladies' and children's clothing, costumes and mantles and, at journey's end, underclothing, positioned both modestly and deliberately so that it was necessary to make a promenade past attractive showcases before achieving such a utilitarian objective.

Through folding doors 'the visitor finds himself [surely 'herself' should also have been mentioned] in the comfortable lounge outside the magnificent café which has been installed for the convenience not only of customers but as an attractive venue where luncheons and teas will be available for the general public.' This was a far cry from the tentative facilities offered at Osborne Street. The lounge, equipped with a public telephone, was intended to be 'a comfortable meeting place, amid delightful surroundings, for customers who will here be able to rest'. The café had an elegant décor of oak panelling and green carpets, an unobtrusive background for an orchestra whose sole aim was to 'discourse sweet music'. Adjoining, more privately, was a gentlemen's smoking room and a ladies' room. In summer, tea would be served on the roof.

On the first floor, too, furniture was displayed in specimen rooms: an ideal small bedroom attached to a lady's boudoir and dressing room furnished in the Chippendale style, a Jacobean lounge, a Jacobean dining room, and a mahogany sitting room. 'The second floor was largely devoted to fine bedroom furnishings in all styles.' Some Hull and East Riding homes no doubt still contain items from the bedroom suites bought at prices ranging from ten to 57 guineas. Although Hammond's were proud of their ability to furnish every size of home, from the cottage to the mansion, most of their customers were somewhere in between. These displays of fashionable furniture educated local taste and provided a tangible aim for those aspiring to join the middle classes.

Victorians and Edwardians were enthusiasts for technical progress. It was a cause for celebration that Hammond's had the largest electric lighting installation in Hull and a system of pneumatic tubes, 'obviating the necessity for the out-of-date cash desks'. Cash was drawn effortlessly up to the counting-house on the first floor and change speedily returned. Thrilling details were provided of the thousands of feet of 'solid drawn brass tubing', bends, sleeves and joints employed in 'one of the largest and most up-to-date plants of its kind in England'. A sign of social change not immediately visible to customers was that there were no longer dormitories for living-in staff.

It was a matter of pride that well-known Hull firms were employed in building and fitting out the new Hammond's, among them Geo. Houlton & Sons, Hollis Bros, King & Co and the National Radiator Company (later Ideal Standard). Amazing to those who remember the building restrictions of the Second World War and its aftermath (which resulted in a lengthy delay before Hammond's could be rebuilt after its destruction in the Blitz), the construction of the store continued after the outbreak of war right up to its opening in 1916 in the midst of terrible news from the Front. A photograph taken on 26 June, 1914, when King George V visited Hull for the official opening of the dock named in his honour shows the store already recognisable but still with much work needed just two months before war was declared.

The transfer of goods from Osborne Street was a major logistic operation and staff were complimented on their valiant work in transferring more than £30,000 worth of stock to the new premises between noon on the Thursday and the Saturday afternoon preceding opening day. On that Saturday afternoon shareholders and the press were given a preview of the premises and enjoyed afternoon tea, 'served in first-class style'.

The day which everyone was waiting for finally arrived, 16 October 1916. 'The doors will be opened and the curtains lifted at 10 o'clock on Monday morning,' was the exciting announcement. Patrons from the past were given a cordial invitation to make a tour of inspection of the new premises, but no one was to feel excluded. There was no question of a grand opening performed by a visiting celebrity. A photograph, however, shows large and orderly ranks of soberly dressed men and women keen to take advantage of the directors' invitation. Sentimentality and nostalgia alone cannot account for the genuine affection local people had for the new store in Paragon Square. It enhanced Hull and they were proud that the city had a place of such splendour. The destruction of the store in 1941 intensified the memories of staff and customers who could boast that they remembered the great days of Hammond's in the inter-war years.

A new face at the new store was that of young Robert Johnson. On 23 October 1916 he began his five-year

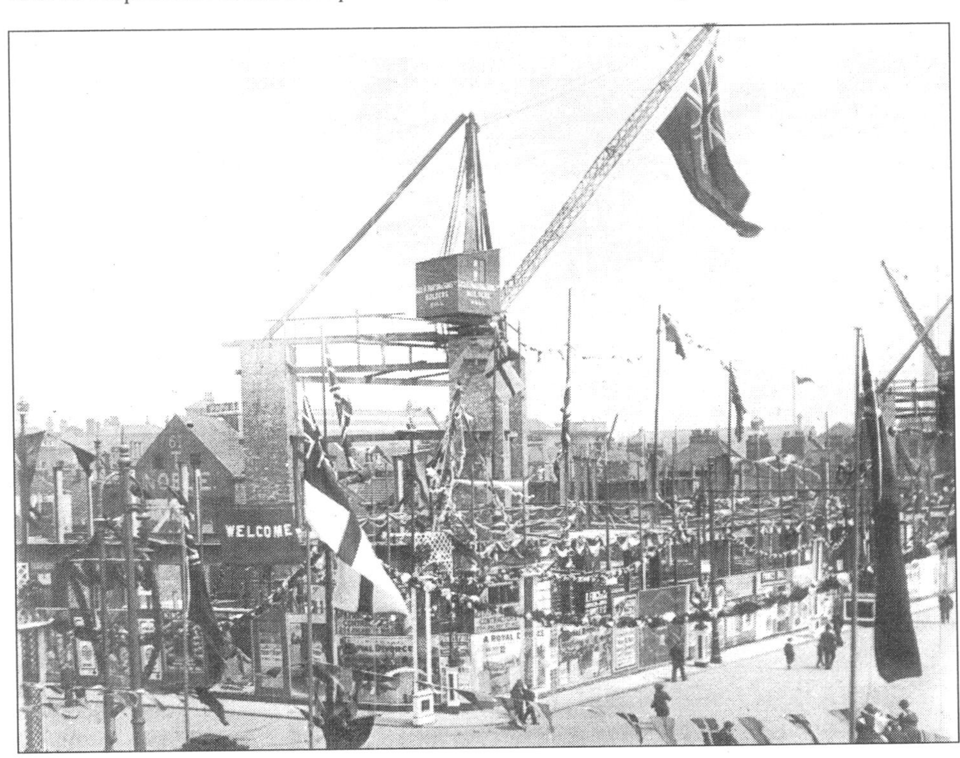

Building work on the new store in Paragon Square.

apprenticeship to the drapery trade, without pay for the first year, then with weekly wages rising from 2s. 6d. to 5s., and finally 10s. in the fifth year. Hammond's were well satisfied with his progress. On the conclusion of the apprenticeship he received a glowing testimonial: 'We have had no fault to find with him, he has always been attentive to business. Good manners with his customers and strictly honest and industrious.' So impressed were his employers that Henry Powell told him that, if he went to Bourne & Hollingsworth for two years' further training, he would be considered for a managerial position. But his father, also Robert, a Beverley man, would not hear of such an outrageous idea. 'If you can't learn it up here you'll not learn it at all.' 'So,' said Robert junior good humouredly when he retired from the Dress Fabrics Department in 1967, 'I've been stuck behind this bloody counter for 50 years.'

The three Powell brothers, William, Henry and Samuel, were now at the head of a more visually impressive enterprise with far greater potential than Osborne Street could ever have possessed and, to assist them they promoted Frank M. Jones, previously a buyer, to be General Manager. In 1916 George G. Griffiths joined James Powell & Sons' Valuation Department. He was, though, supportive of every aspect of Hammond's activities and in 1930 was appointed Secretary of the company on the retirement of Mr. Lehar. One of his achievements was introducing the staff welfare system and guiding its progress until he retired in 1952.

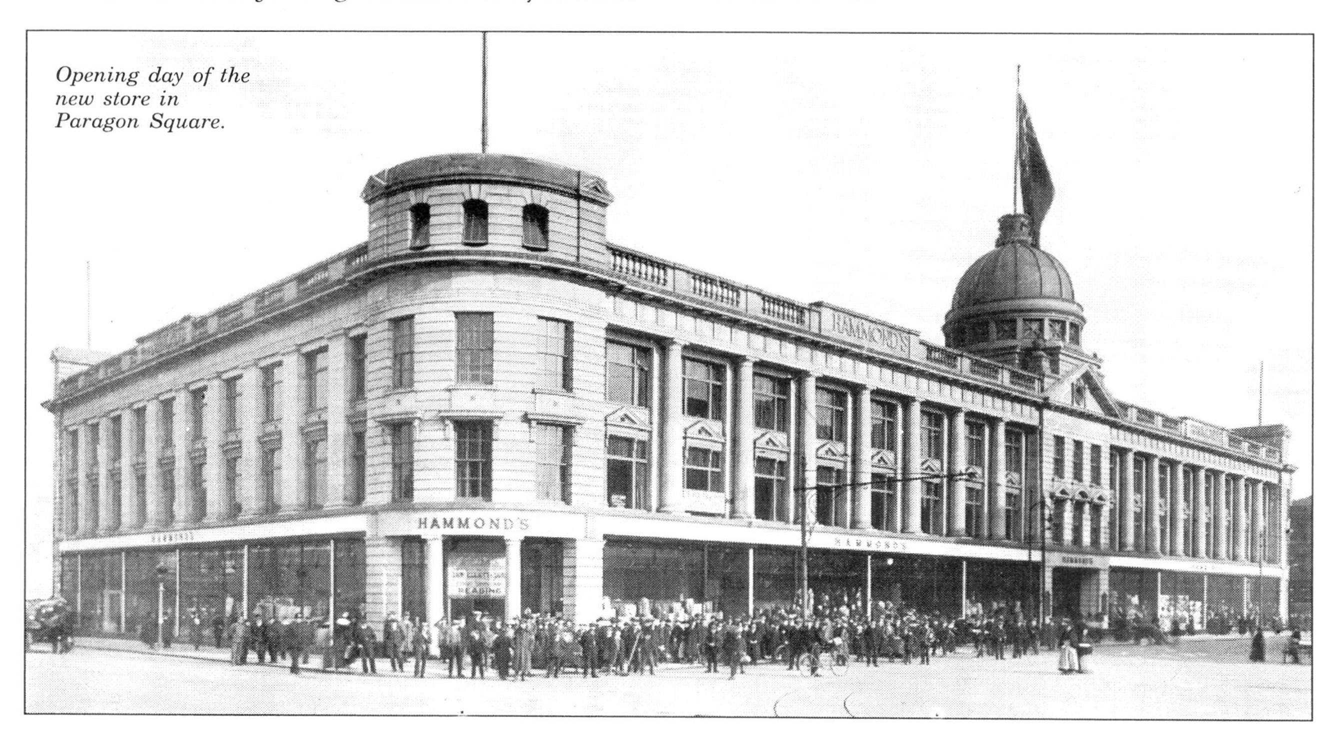

Opening day of the new store in Paragon Square.

4

The Post-War Years

The war which some had expected to finish by Christmas 1914 dragged on for four years of suffering and death, but, to universal relief and rejoicing, the end came on 11 November 1918. James Powell (born 1898), son of William, was one of those released from the forces, and, after training in Manchester, joined the company in 1919 as buyer and Assistant Manager. A future Chairman, he was the instigator of many of the improvements of the 1930s, in particular the installation of an escalator, the creation of the domed ballroom and the re-shaping of the fashion showrooms. A sign that a third generation of Powells was gaining ground was James's 21st birthday on 29 December 1919. Seventy of the oldest members of staff, all previously at Osborne Street, presented him with a bureau which his father had 'very kindly selected'.

Another major figure in the Hammond's story joined the company in 1919. Arthur Hall had been a living-in-trainee with Cockayne's of Sheffield, before returning to join his father, who had a draper's shop in Hessle. Trade there was too slow for his liking so he sold up and joined Hammond's as a traveller, visiting customers all over the district, in particular the farming community, between whom and the store he built up a happy relationship. Later he was appointed Manager of the ironmongery shop which Hammond's had opened in the Garden Village Centre. It was a brave attempt to move into a new market but it did not prove a profitable venture, it was eventually closed and Mr. Hall became buyer of dress materials. On the death of Frank Jones in 1937 he was appointed Staff Manager and, shortly after, combined this with the duties of General Manager, a position he held until his retirement in 1957.

Hammond's angled their post-war publicity to the mood which prevailed after the ending of a war which had brought so much suffering. 'Wander round in **Peace** – You will not be asked to buy,' Hammond's invited their customers in a large formal advertisement of 1919 in which three ladies in the latest fashions posed elegantly between tall wreathed columns while at their feet doves hovered around a banner bearing the quotation, 'Universal peace lies like a shaft of light across the land.'

Hammond's proclaimed their marketing manifesto: 'Our policy in Peace-time is the same as it was in War-time. We entered our New Premises at a time of great national stress, but we set out with a firm determination to overcome difficulties and to carry out our pre-war programme. The clouds are now behind us, and we take this opportunity of thanking the public of Hull for backing us in our enterprise during the years of war that are passed. In this year of glorious Victory we look forward with hope for a further expansion of business, knowing that as the restrictions on trade are being removed one by one, we can supply all your needs from a choice of the best materials on the market.'

In June 1920 Hammond's issued the first edition of a house magazine – how long it lasted is not known – as a more effective method of communication than the familiar notices in places where staff congregated. The principal item in this new publication was a paternalistic message from the Chairman: his subject, Efficiency. 'A big business such as ours,' he wrote, 'has become like a machine.' All parties had to work in unison and a failure in one department rebounded on the whole organisation. It would, for example, be pointless to please a customer by efficient service at the point of sale but later cause annoyance by careless and slovenly packing of her parcel or non-delivery at the promised time. William Powell hastened to point out that he was not casting any aspersions on the Despatch Department: this was entirely a suppositional case.

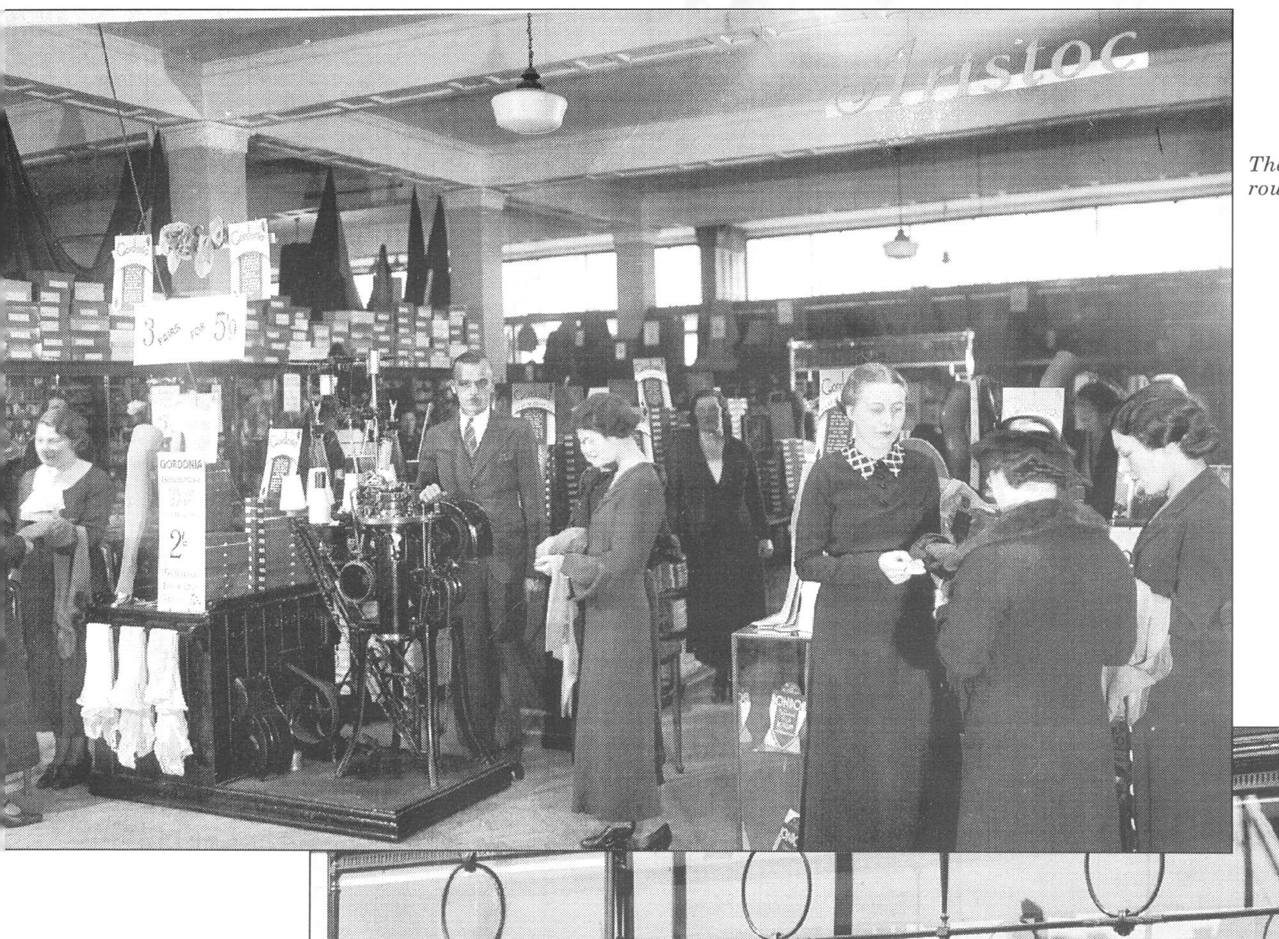

The new walk-round store.

A window display. The plaque, rescued after the Blitz, is on the staircase wall of the present store.

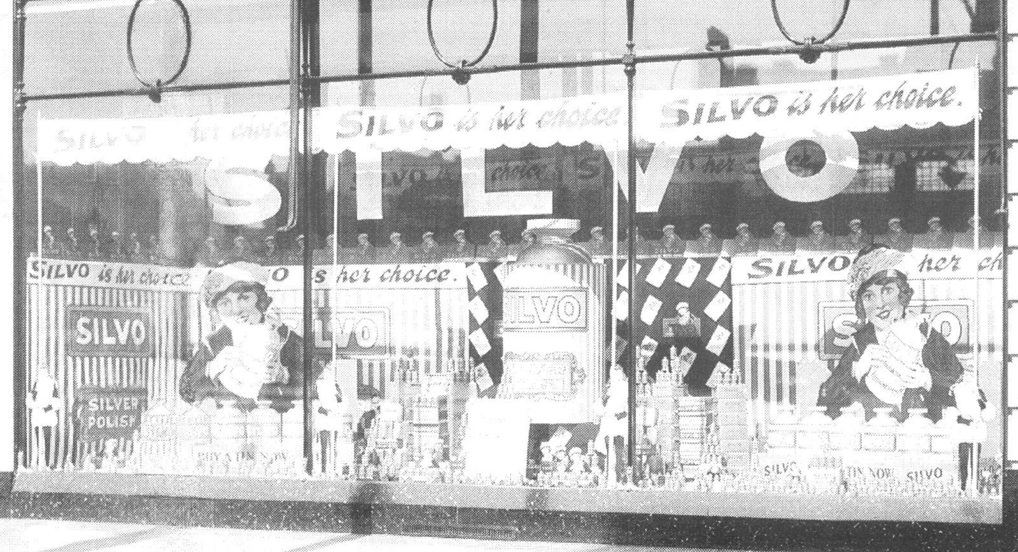

His whole message was morally uplifting: 'Remember always that, however humble may be your position, it is important that your work should be well done. Customers should always be able to say, "I like going to Hammond's because the assistants are always so reliable, capable and obliging." To have worked at Hammond's should be a sufficient guarantee of efficiency when applying for a situation elsewhere.' He ended with a quotation from *Hamlet:* 'This above all, To thine own self be true . . .'

The contents of the magazine accorded with the ethos of the time. Pleasure was expressed at the announcement of a bonus, an indication both of successful trading and of the directors' appreciation of the efforts of their staff. Important new rules were introduced affecting pass-out checks and staff purchases, but two-way communication was still in its infancy. It was noted with sorrow that the suggestion box was neglected and apathy had made the staff committee virtually defunct. Perhaps Hammond's were aspiring to royal patronage: it was reported that the Queen had 'sent a nice letter of thanks to the directors for the copy of the Wool Booklet which had been sent to her'.

The jollity and heartiness of the social and personal news items were rather forced. The Whist Club had been given an Irishman's rise by demotion to the Third Division; it was hoped that Miss Stephenson of Haberdashery, who had gained 70 marks in the soprano section of the Hull Musical Competition, would one day perform for the benefit of her colleagues; Mr. Harper was gradually gaining strength and weight and hoped soon to be back at business

1821 100 YEARS 1921

A CENTURY AGO the business of HAMMOND'S was commenced in a small shop near the North Bridge. Under the patronage of the inhabitants of Hull & the East Riding it has developed until it is now one of the largest & most important in the Provinces.

THE FINANCIAL YEAR which just closes HAS BEEN THE BIGGEST AND MOST SUCCESSFUL in the history of the firm and the Directors feel that to inaugurate the CENTENARY they would like to express their appreciation of the support received during the time the business has been under their control, in a practical form

IT HAS THEREFORE BEEN DECIDED THAT ON

TUESDAY & WEDNESDAY

NEXT 8 & 9 FEBRUARY

the WHOLE of their VALUABLE STOCKS *(with the exception of those goods where the prices are fixed by the Makers or by Trade Agreement and also the Food sold in the Restaurant)* will be offered for Sale at

ONE HALF THE MARKED PRICES

All the Stock is marked in plain figures at the usual cash prices, and whether the purchase is a piece of tape at 1d or a Suite of Furniture at £200, half the price will be charged. The Stock can be inspected now but no goods will be sold at half price except between 9 a.m. and 6 p.m. on the days mentioned

ALL GOODS MUST BE PAID FOR AT TIME OF PURCHASE. NO CREDIT CAN BE GIVEN on this occasion.

CELEBRATE THE CENTENARY BY MAKING A PURCHASE

HAMMOND'S Ltd PARAGON SQUARE HULL

The great sale of 1921.

('Cheer up, Ted, old chappie, we very much miss you.'), while Miss Nicholson (Boots), Miss Chapman (Art Needlework) and Miss Lane (Despatch) had resigned on taking up 'important positions in the matrimonial world'. (When a woman married she had to make a formal request to continue her employment and, if this was agreed, her name was published in the staff magazine.) One piece of information makes the heart sink. Mr Brooks, it was noted, possessed a very interesting and excellent collection of snap shots taken during his time abroad: 'They are really well worth seeing.'

The great sale of 1921.

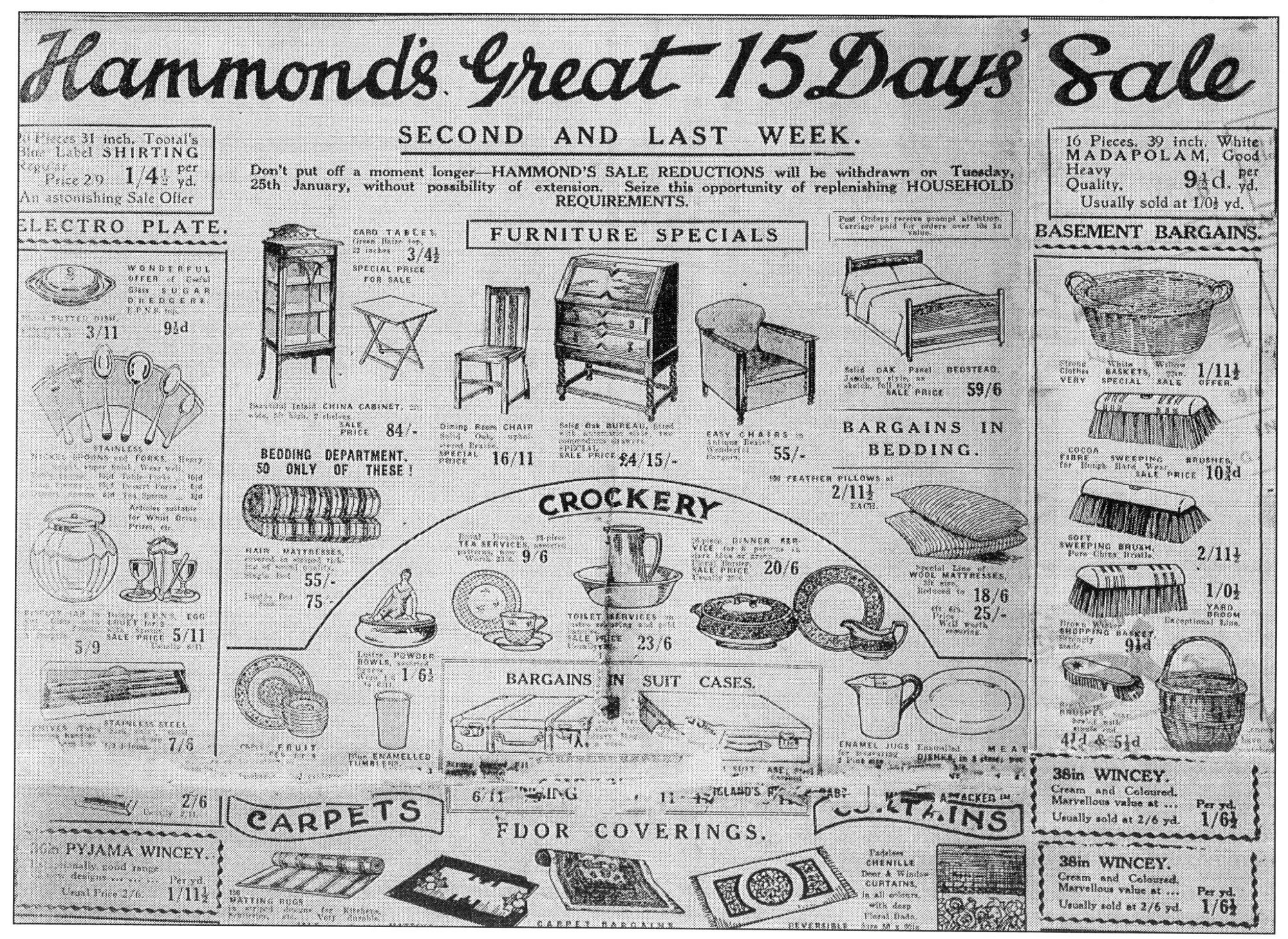

In the euphoric reaction to the ending of a war which had seemed endless there was a boom in retail trade. But this bubble soon burst. By 1921 prices had begun dropping rapidly, stocks had to be marked down and great losses were feared. Hammond's, however, plucked triumph out of potential disaster. By happy chance 1921 was the centenary of the year which had always been accepted as the date when H. W. Hammond had founded his business. It was an anniversary worth celebrating and Hammond's took advantage of this fortuitous coincidence by organising a two-day sale with everything at half-price, to customers an unprecedented gesture of generosity but for Hammond's a clever ploy to put money into the bank and obtain a breathing space before new stocks were purchased at lower prices.

In a speech to Hull Rotary Club in 1963 Samuel Powell's son, John, by then Chairman, described the 1921 sale as the turning point in the history of the company. Prospects had looked bleak, prices continued to fall and it required real courage to sell at such low prices. 'I have wondered,' he said, 'whether in similar circumstances today we should be so courageous in adversity.' At the time of the sale he was at school but he heard about it from his elders. Apart from achieving its objectives, it had in his opinion, produced a priceless asset: 'its publicity value lasted for years'.

It was a success passing all expectations. A queue formed round the building in the early hours of the morning and, after the first rush of customers had filled it to its maximum capacity, the doors had to be closed, new customers being admitted only when others left. The future Mrs Dorothea Park, then newly engaged, was enticed by the publicity. Fifty years later she recalled, 'I went hopefully but, seeing the miles of queues, decided it was hopeless. Some friends had a front stand at the middle door in Jameson Street. I stopped to have a word with them. Almost immediately the doors were opened and the crowd surged forward and I was thrust into the shop bruised and breathless. The pressure cracked the right-hand side window from top to bottom. I was not a buyer – I felt so awful I went straight out of the end door and home, where it was discovered I had a broken rib.'

Two years later, in 1923, came the death at his Beverley Road home of the second of James Powell's sons, Henry. Aged only 57, he had been away from business for some time. His obituary described him as a sound, shrewd businessman whose wise advice was widely sought, and who had been very prominent in the Hull Drapers' Association and the Hull Chamber of Trade. But there were more personal, affectionate tributes. To some he was Saint Henry, a great personality, a lovable man, generous and hospitable of whom everyone was fond. He reminded one former employee of a Dickens character, always jolly and enjoying his pinch of snuff. In his £27,485 will he was generous to his family, his personal staff and to those who had helped in making Hammond's such a success. A long list of old employees received £25 each and his two brothers and Frank Jones were each bequeathed 1,000 £1 Ordinary Shares in the company.

Inflationary changes to the value of money have made prices from the past meaningless without reference to contemporary wage levels. The goods on offer, however, give a glimpse of a domestic lifestyle still vivid in older people's memories, far more labour-intensive than anything experienced today. Basement bargains in the January 1927 sale were strong white willow clothes baskets, cocoa fibre sweeping brushes, scrubbing brushes and coal savers – fire bricks to fit inside the grate and reduce the amount of fuel consumed. For kitchens and sculleries 'very durable' matting rugs were available in striped designs, and, for the bedroom, hair mattresses 'covered in striped stitching of sound quality' and wincey pyjamas. More

Staff outing (now owned by the son of Eva Thornham, who joined the staff in 1919) and took part in this outing.

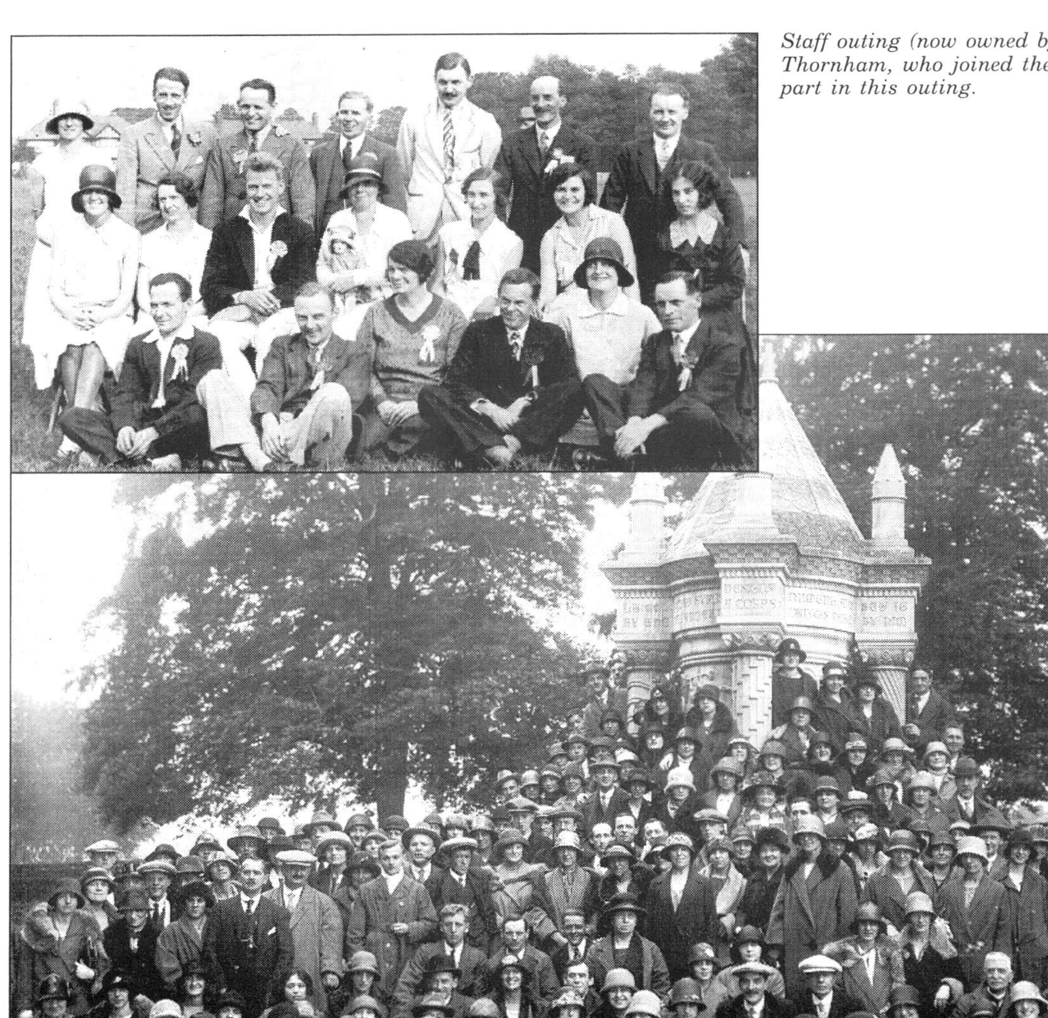

Staff outing, Sledmere.

luxurious, for the more affluent, were stylish items likely to arouse the envy of less fortunate neighbours: a lustre powder bowl surmounted by a female in an unrevealing bathing costume, a cut-glass biscuit jar with EPNS frame, a dainty egg cruet, also EPNS, and, for those who had the money to spare, a beautiful inlaid cabinet, price 84s., in which to show off one's china.

A catalogue (undated but of the same period) for a 15-day half-yearly sale covered the whole range of Hammond's goods at bargain prices and with patterns of material sent out post free. A limited number of gramophones and Marconi wireless sets, either soiled or second-hand, were offered at prices which emphasise that, in its early days, radio was a luxury which only the better-off could afford; one originally at £18. 6s., for example, was reduced to £10. 10s. Every title of Columbia Records was in stock.

At that time Hammond's operated a second-hand furniture department in West Street but, for those who preferred new, it was possible to furnish a home out of income by asking for Hammond's terms. If the massive reductions were not enough inducement, there was also the opportunity to hear the orchestra playing in the restaurant each day from 12 noon to 2 pm and from 3.30 pm to 5.30 pm.

5

The 1930s

For country people a day in Hull was a major undertaking and a visit to Hammond's a memorable experience. Bob Wrightson spent his childhood in Goodmanham. Three or four times a year from 1929 to the outbreak of war he was taken by his mother on a shopping expedition to Hull, an outing which began with a 1½ mile walk to Market Weighton station for the train journey to Hull. As they left Paragon Station he was always a little scared by the statues of soldiers on the war memorial and very conscious of the number of children running around in bare feet. The high spot of the day was a leisurely lunch in Hammond's restaurant serenaded by a three- or four-piece orchestra led by a slim bespectacled violinist.

At Christmas there was the added thrill of spectacular displays in the toy department: grottoes, Father Christmas and model train layouts at which he gazed boggle-eyed. Now living in York, Mr Wrightson still has a Hornby locomotive 'which Father Christmas brought me from that wonderland'. In these halcyon years of public transport he recalls a regular Saturday evening shopping train from Market Weighton to Hull, returning from Paragon Station at around 9.30 pm, all for 1s. 9d. (8.75p). Satisfied Hammond's customers are always happy to boast of the longevity of the goods they purchased. Mr Wrightson has in his garage a cupboard which formed part of a bedroom suite bought at Hammond's in the 1930s.

Hammond's were always proud of their reputation for wool and obviously invested considerable time and money in producing instruction guides to attract customers. One, on rug making, is a substantial publication with detailed technical information, all fully illustrated and with articles by authorities on various aspects of the subject, even on suggestions for colour coordination in interior design. An incident which turned out to be less serious than at first it appeared was an early morning fire in the wool stock department in the basement in February 1930. Dense clouds of yellowish fumes and smoke quickly filled a great portion of the building and staff arriving for work had to wait in West Street. It was quickly dealt with and normality restored.

Another break with the past came through the sudden death of Samuel, the youngest of the three brothers, in 1933, again at a relatively young age, 62. Although he did not follow his father into public life, he had always taken an active role in the firm, he was well-known in business circles and connected with the furnishing trades section of the Chamber of Trade. A hale and hearty man, outside business he was a freemason and enjoyed shooting. At the age of 41 he married 19-year-old Mary Wilson and at the time of his death was living at The Bungalow, Cottingham the former pied à terre of C. H. Wilson M.P., later Lord Nunburnholme, and now Hull University's Cleminson Hall. Staff included a butler and housekeeper and Mr and Mrs Samuel Powell were great entertainers. 'I can very truthfully say that he was very well loved by his family, many friends and all his associates at business,' was his son John's simple and sincere tribute. John got to know his father particularly well when he accompanied him on a three-month trip to South Africa after completing an apprenticeship in London.

It was always considered preferable for future executives to gain experience outside the family business, and on 1 July 1927 John Powell had entered into a three-year apprenticeship with the firm of Oetzmann & Co Ltd of 67-85 Hampstead Road, London, 'to learn the Art, Trade or Business of Complete Home Furnishing and the general departmental organization and routine thereof'. His father, Samuel, a party to the indenture, paid a premium of £250, part to be repaid to his son in three rising instalments: £40 the first year, then £60 and finally £80. For his part of the bargain John agreed to keep his employers' secrets, observe their lawful commands, refrain from damaging their goods and undertake a whole host of subsidiary promises.

In July 1930, on the completion of the three years, John asked if he could gain some experience in the carpet department. Oetzmann's suggested a minimum period of four months, as there was a great deal to learn, for a salary at the same rate as for his final year's apprenticeship and he took up his further period of work experience from September to Christmas. Apparently he fulfilled all the commitments he had undertaken. On 31 January 1931 his indenture was endorsed: 'We hereby certify that the within named John Wilson Powell has well and faithfully served the full period of his apprenticeship in accordance with the terms of the written Deed.' A director of Oetzmann's also added a personal note: 'With my hearty good wishes for a future both happy and prosperous.' In 1931 he joined Hammond's as assistant buyer in the furniture department and took over that section on the death of his father.

The possible financial disasters resulting from the Depression began to recede and in 1933 Hammond's felt able to gain much needed extra space by adding a fourth floor to the building, which in turn allowed them to introduce an important new feature, the Dome Ballroom, fated to have its brief period of glory but, until its wartime destruction, a centre of Hull's social life with a glittering succession of dances, dinners and functions night after night during the winter season.

James Powell, son of William, and Arthur Hall were key figures in organising these events and, though all seemed smoothly effortless to those who danced the night away, behind the scenes it was regarded as 'one of

James Powell, grandson of the founder.

The Dome Ballroom.

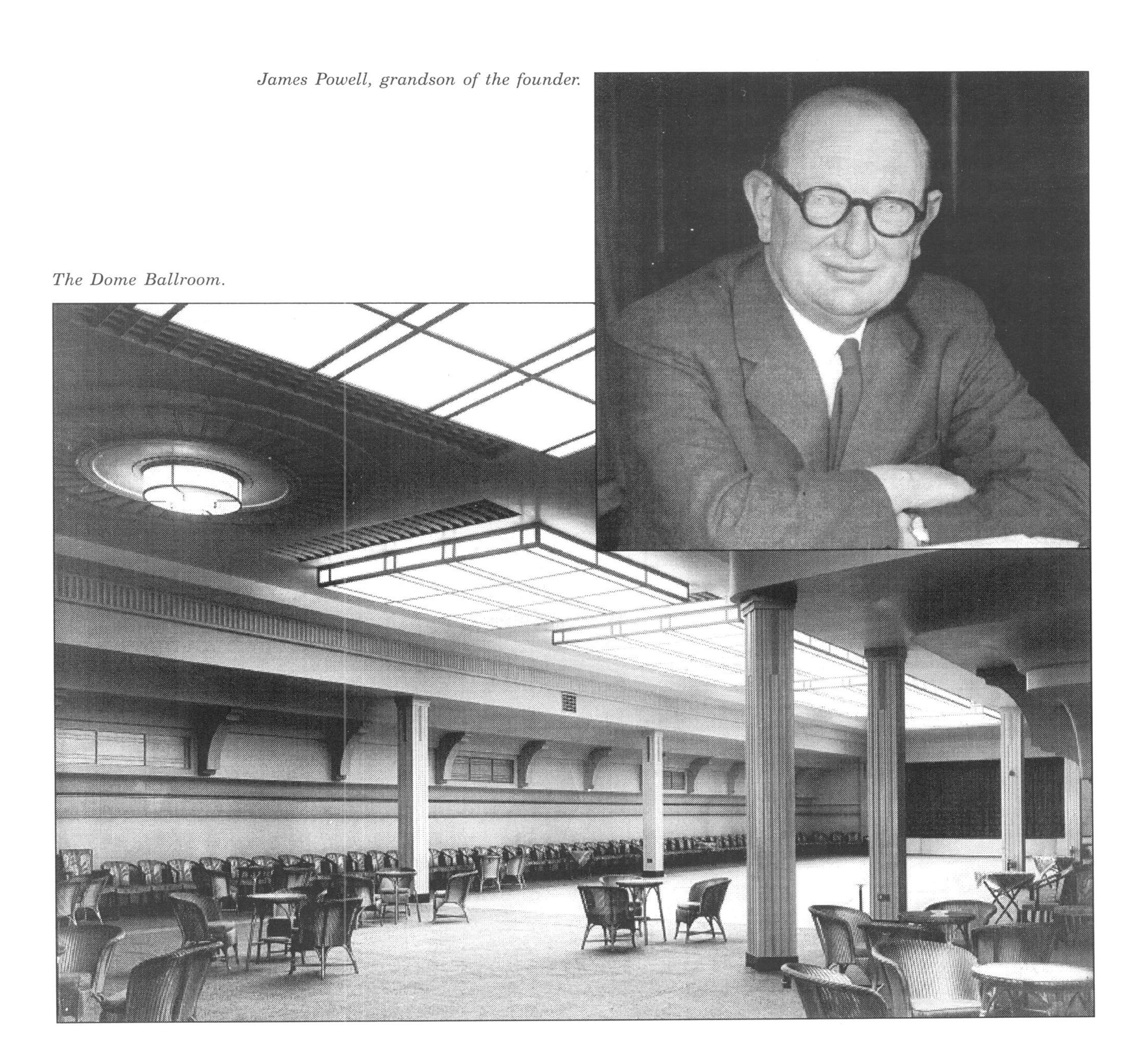

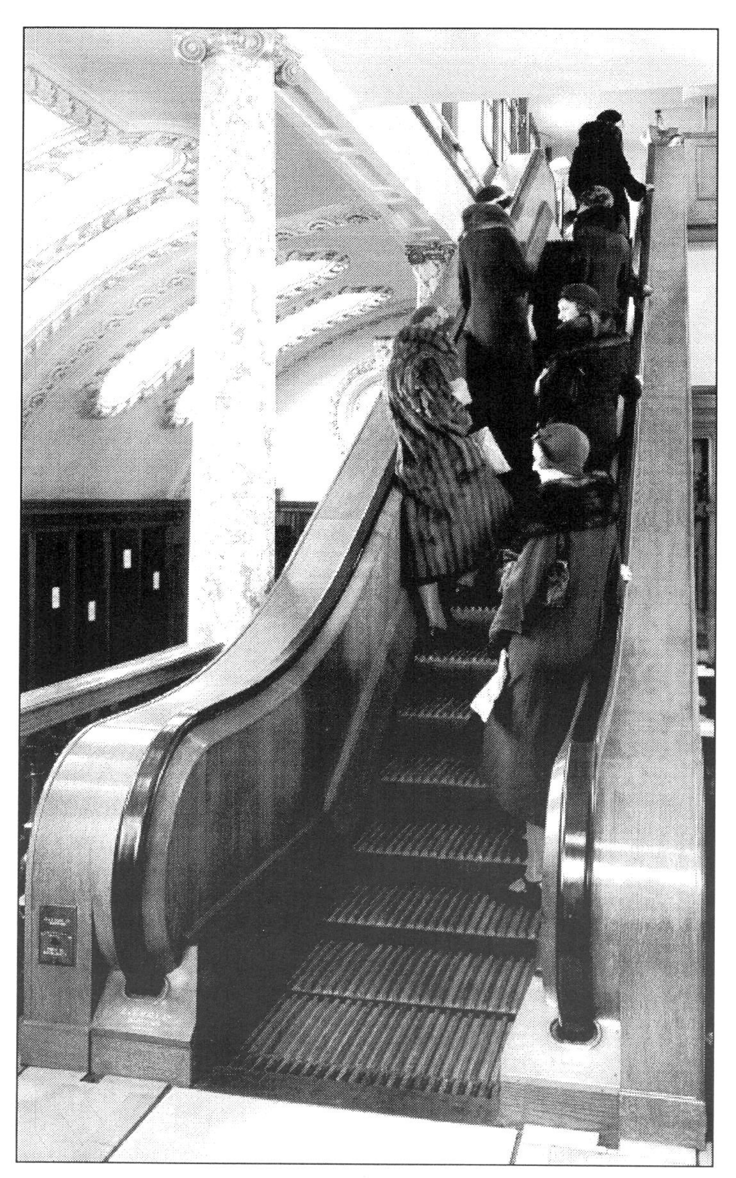

A new experience for Hull shoppers.

the biggest administrative headaches' that Hammond's had ever experienced. The other half of the new floor provided a spacious location for gardens, laid out artistically by Backhouse's of York, and garden furniture in summer; for the toy department and Father Christmas in winter.

An innovation which excited much interest in Hull was the installation in 1936 of an escalator, the first in the city and one of the first in the North. As people were so unused to such a contraption, a commissionaire was posted at both foot and head of the escalator to ensure safety: less cautious than Harrods, who had not only a commissionaire but also a nursing sister at the top to administer brandy and sal volatile.

Attracting less attention but probably more crucial to the efficient running of the business was the new building which went up in West Street around the same time for housing stock and for handling Hammond's' extensive postal trade, particularly in wool. It was to come into its own, in a way never intended, after the destruction of the main building in the Blitz of 1941.

The passing of time means that the oldest recollections of staff and customers tend to be of the later inter-war years. Mrs Mary Mawer, for example, worked in the Paragon Square store from 1936 to 1941, when she left to get married. She started on a weekly wage of 10s., which eventually rose to £1. 2s. 6d. Wages were supplemented by commission but a strict order of precedence prevailed and, with 1st, 2nd and 3rd Sales having prior rights of access to customers, there was little chance for a junior. She was a timid youngster and found it a struggle to acquire a half-crown rise. William Powell she thought a nice man, James always looked forbidding, while John, her superior, was charming. All the females wore black. Male commissionaires, lift attendants and bell boys were attractively uniformed in cream trousers with blue and silver buttons, except in winter when the colour was blue.

The glass roof to the top floor created a hot environment for those, like herself, working among the summer displays of garden furniture, though the gardens themselves were a delight. One year a waterfall cascaded over rocks, and tropical birds – for sale – flew about in an aviary. In winter it became the Christmas fair. Most memorable was the year when the Tower of London was the theme, with stalls decorated in an appropriate olde-worlde style. A group of girls went to Madame Sharah, a well-known drama teacher, to perfect their dancing skills so that they could perform throughout the day on a raised platform, as pirates, farmyard animals or soldiers from the past. The scenic ride to Father Christmas cost 6d. and the gifts he handed out (which she had helped to pack) were of good value. On sale were Christmas trees from Germany, and glass and baubles from Japan. Representatives from Sunday Schools would buy quantities of books as prizes for their pupils at what were then well-attended organisations.

At one mannequin display in the ballroom there was a lull in proceedings before the dramatic finale of the entrance of the bride in full wedding regalia. Young Mary, entranced by the spectacle, was leaning against an umbrella stand. The silence was shattered when it collapsed, leaving her struggling beneath it. The sales were eagerly awaited local events. Everything was reduced in price and Mrs Mawer remembers only one occasion when cheap crockery was bought in as an attraction. Before the sales started there was a massive mailing of brochures to customers, including some overseas. Extra staff were employed for contacting these distant people and samples of such merchandise as stationery and wool despatched. Hammond's had always operated a flourishing mail-order business, and the excellent postal services of those days enabled it to function with great efficiency.

The common theme of all former staff's recollections of the inter-war years is the happy atmosphere of the store, very much a family concern with the Powells, never remote executives, taking an active interest in everything. Rules were strictly enforced but this tended, as it usually does, to encourage a team spirit.

Mrs Joan Marshall, who describes it as 'a beautiful shop – *the* shop of Hull', where her sister Enid, was in the restaurant, worked as a junior in the pots and pans department in the basement. Once again the strict order of precedence, Miss Winn as 1st Sales, Miss Freeman 2nd and herself, then Joan Hellings, 3rd, meant there were few opportunities for serving potentially high-spending customers, though once, she recalls, she did manage to earn a penny commission. The *esprit de corps* extended into leisure time. Mrs Marshall won a silver cup in a ladies' amateur race in 1939 (which she still has, though she was bombed three times) and is now amused to think of herself on a Thursday afternoon, when the store was closed, biking to Cottingham to play hockey. 'There was plenty of social life,' she says.

Similar happy memories come from Mrs Audrey Lynch. She joined Hammond's when she left school, aged 15, working first in soft furnishings, later in toys and leaving only when the building was destroyed in the Blitz. It was a family shop in every sense of the word. Not only were two generations of Powells fully involved but her brother also worked for Hammond's, serving his apprenticeship as a French polisher and upholsterer until the outbreak of war.

One sorrow of this period was the death of a highly respected member of the Hammond's team, Frank M. Jones, who had joined the firm at Osborne Street in 1903. He had previously been away from work for some time and, on 1 July 1937, returning from a buying trip, collapsed on King's Cross Station, dying soon after.

In retrospect these final years before the Second World War seem a golden age. There were still great poverty and massive social problems but the years of Depression had been weathered, there were clear signs of economic progress, slum property was being replaced by far superior council housing, suburbia was growing, and owning a mortgaged semi with all mod cons, a garden and sometimes even a car was now a realistic ambition for many.

Hull was a city of smart shops occupying impressive buildings and there was a mass of entertainment on offer. From the early years of the century Hull people had been pioneering film fans, the cinemas in the city centre (some with cafés) were attractive venues for a self-indulgent treat and there was live entertainment for all tastes at the various theatres, the Alexandra, the Palace and the Tivoli as well as the prestigious Little Theatre (later the New Theatre), a breeding ground for future stars of stage and screen. Before or after the performances Powolny's Restaurant in King Edward Street provided fine cuisine and glamour for those who could afford the best. Hammond's in particular benefited from the opening, in 1931, of Ferensway, cutting through a mass of small streets and making its corner position even more prominent. Hammond's looked towards Europe. Hull gave easy access to the Netherlands and Hammond's regularly displayed their goods at exhibitions in Amsterdam, the Hague and Rotterdam.

A major objective of this period was for Hammond's to be identified as a fashion store as well as one dealing in household items. In the year in which war was declared a Modern Fashion Department, complete with furniture, displays, fitting rooms and concealed lighting had been installed on the first floor. 'There were wonderful showrooms,' one former employee, Mrs Marjorie Perry (née Stockdale) recalls. 'Acres and acres of lovely carpets – and the wool counters seemed to go on for miles.' She joined Hammond's as a temporary salesgirl on leaving school, spending whole days in West

Hull Publicity Club's Dinner and Dance, 8 January 1936. The chef was John Snow.

PROGRAMME

1	Quickstep	Half and Half
2	Waltz	Love Me for Ever
	DINNER - 8-30 p.m.	
3	Foxtrot	You are My Lucky Star
4	Veleta	Musical Comedy
5	Paul Jones	Medley
6	Waltz	As Long as our Hearts are Young
7	Palais Glide	Sing-Song
8	Foxtrot	On Treasure Island
9	Naval Three-Step	Cavalcade
10	Waltz	Alice Blue Gown
11	Quickstep	That's a Plenty
12	Paul Jones	Medley
13	Old Time Waltz	Naughty Marietta
14	Palais Glide	Community Songs
15	Foxtrot	After all These Years
16	Musical Switch	Selected
17	Veleta	The Duck Song
18	Foxtrot	Broadway Rhythm
19	Naval Three-Step	All Hands on Deck
20	Quick Step	Tiger Rag
21	Waltz	Goodnight

MANLEY'S ORCHESTRA.

M.C.—MR. F. EUSTACE.

WEST END STUDIOS — CABARET.

MENU

Hors d'oeuvres a la Riche

Consomme Andalouse
Cream of Vegetables

Fried Lemon Sole with Tartare Sauce

Roast Turkey with Stuffing and Sausage
Vegetables of the Season

Christmas Pudding with Rum Sauce
Sherry Trifle
Bombe Carmen
Petit Fours

Coffee

Salted Almonds

Catering by
HAMMOND'S Limited.

Wines, etc., by
MOORS' & ROBSON'S
Limited.

Street despatching sales literature and patterns to the many customers who lived outside Hull. Once the sales started she was attached to a specific department and was kept busy running with cash to the cash desk – presumably the pneumatic tubes were overwhelmed by excessive demand – though not allowed to serve.

Later she started an apprenticeship at Bloom's in Brook Street but was often sent to Hammond's for material. It was a red-letter day when Jessie Matthews, earlier one of Cochrane's Young Ladies and then at the height of her fame, came in 1938 to present Hammond's with a silver cup and a cheque for their Display Department's success in winning the National Window Competition for Sylmara Fabrics. The public turned up in their thousands, giving the police a considerable headache, and Marjorie, as keen as people were in those pre-television days to see someone famous, was allowed to go out on a dubious errand to share the excitement. The stand on which she perched to get a better view fell apart. Back at Bloom's she came in for a lot of teasing. Mr Powell, her colleagues pretended, had been on the phone and wanted compensation.

That year Christmas came early to Hammond's, as the opening of the top-floor Christmas Bazaar, the mecca for shoppers, especially those accompanied by children, was timed to coincide with Jessie Matthews' visit to take advantage of the huge numbers of spectators easily enticeable into the building. As a memento of this happy event, John Powell kept a signed photograph of Jessie Matthews on his desk for many years.

A long article, 'Hammond's of Hull, A Century of Retail Service', which appeared in the January 1939 edition of a national journal, *Store and Shop Management,* was something its author never intended: the swansong of a city, a store and a way of life which were soon to be transformed by the disastrous impact of war.

Hull was proud of its status as the country's Third Port (and its claim to be the cheapest), with 13 miles of quays and a river frontage of seven miles and as a great manufacturing centre standing on one of England's largest rivers, the Humber. And in this thriving city Hammond's was the most favourably placed store. On postcards of Paragon Square it always formed a conspicuous background.

Although the article was aimed at the cognoscenti of retailing, the passing of time has made it a period piece, a record of the store at its pre-war peak of prosperity. Details are recorded which might otherwise have been forgotten or overlooked. Hammond's name, for example, was incorporated into the structure of the building, relief lettering on stone blocks standing out with clarity and dignity.

The new floor with dormer windows set into sloping sides had been added so skilfully in 1933 it seems likely that such an extension had been foreseen by the original planners. Hammond's' reputation as a pioneer of new ideas in retailing was corroborated by the writer's comments: 'I found many apparently modern developments had been in use here for a number of years.' The interior layout adopted for the previous 20 years by Hammond's had recently been hailed as an innovation when it was introduced into a West End store. Instead of the customary central aisle with entrances to departments on either side, Hammond's had two main corridors parallel with the main (Jameson Street) frontage. Between them, departments were arranged in a series of nine bays so that shoppers passing up and down the broad aisles on either side could enter or pass the departments at will.

Good communication in the form of personal contact between directors and customers had always been a principle underlying the store's trading activities. Executives were not hidden away in some remote region but had their offices in the centre of the ground floor, where they were easily accessible to customers and buyers: 'Whenever an executive leaves his office he has to pass up one of the main avenues of customer circulation, where he is recognised and acknowledged by regular shoppers.'

There was a glowing description of the ballroom on the top floor. It was suffused with light, both natural and artificial, by a sophisticated system incorporating 'a laylight of Thermolax glass'. When music was needed the orchestra would play from a stage at the end of the room, which at other times offered a perfect setting for mannequin parades. Furniture occupied most of the second floor but there was also a ladies' hairdressing department (where the 'Christy wave' had been introduced), fitted with 12 cubicles, and a restaurant seating 130, an adjunct to the main restaurant on the floor below, which seated 350. Both served a 1s. 9d. three-course lunch. Efforts to improve facilities never ceased. Now that the extensive improvements to the fashion department had been completed, plans were in hand to obtain more space on both first and second floors 'by building out over a portion of the roof adjoining the dome over the well in the centre of the building'.

Praise was given for the way carpets were displayed by 'the Neeson system of hanging', which enabled them to be turned over like the pages of a book, a convenience for customers, who could inspect a large stock in a small space of time, and for staff, who were spared the heavy work of hauling and lifting necessary when carpets were shown on the floor.

As for the much-vaunted escalator, still a great novelty, contrary to the usual practice it did not begin on the ground floor but linked first and second floors. There was just one escalator, controlled by switches; during busy times it was kept moving in an upward direction, reversed towards closing time, and, during quieter periods, immediately after opening in the morning and at lunchtime, stopped altogether and used as an ordinary staircase.

Secretary G. G. Griffiths confirmed that Hammond's relied on a regular clientele of middle-class customers and that the directors' policy was to maintain solid progression in all the main departments, avoiding the 'stunts' and the 'little shops' which their contemporaries were adopting. Ironically, specialist shops within the store were to become a prominent feature in the post-war period.

For their expertise in wool Hammond's had acquired a national, even an international, reputation. In the West Street building, purposely constructed for the storage and despatch of wool, 70 packers would be employed during sales: 'The wool counter in the centre of the store and the stock fixture behind it are the largest in the country devoted to this class of merchandise.'

Hammond's were one of the forerunners of a new method of retailing when they replaced the usual monotonous rows of boxes in the shoe department by displays of shoes in illuminated cases. Stocks were kept unobtrusive but easily accessible. An X-ray machine was available for confirmation of fittings – an innovation which shops later abandoned in the light of medical worries.

Another sign of changing times was an internal broadcasting system. Every day at about 3.30 pm special attractions were announced. The fleet of 12 Morris vans which made deliveries over a 30-mile area had, in 1939, been augmented by a 'junior unit' for shorter journeys and auxiliary service: the Rytecraft Scootertruck small-scale delivery vans put Hammond's into the forefront of experimentation as the first store in the country to try out these vehicles.

'Hammond's', concluded the article, 'is the first building upon which the eye of every arrival in Hull by the "iron road" alights, and its fine run of brightly lighted windows is one of the last visual memories carried away by the departing visitor. On that unique and most favoured site Hammond's serves veritably as one of the portals of Kingston-upon-Hull.'

6

War

The declaration of war on 3 September 1939 did not have the same sudden impact on a peaceful world as that of 1914. Many had foreseen that war was inevitable; the only doubt was when it would begin. Well before September there were frightening signs of the coming conflict. Air raid shelters and first aid posts were established, black-outs prepared, fire-fighting equipment made ready, sandbags placed in position and practice given in the use of gas masks and in coping with extreme emergencies. In West Street, Hammond's built an air raid shelter to house 600 staff. When raids started, the weird, unmistakable sound of the warning siren made the basement a much-used place of refuge; everyone seemed to consider it one of the best air-raid shelters in Hull.

Yet, once the official announcement had been made, the first months were a strange period of 'phoney war', when expected calamities failed to happen and some were lulled into a false sense of security; others prepared themselves for an onslaught which they were certain would come. Dunkirk, the Battle of Britain and the grim reality of total war were still in the future when Hammond's announced their 15-day sale in January 1940.

At the beginning of the war Hammond's had between 750 and 800 staff. Over 150 now received their calling-

The store was blitzed on 7 May 1941.

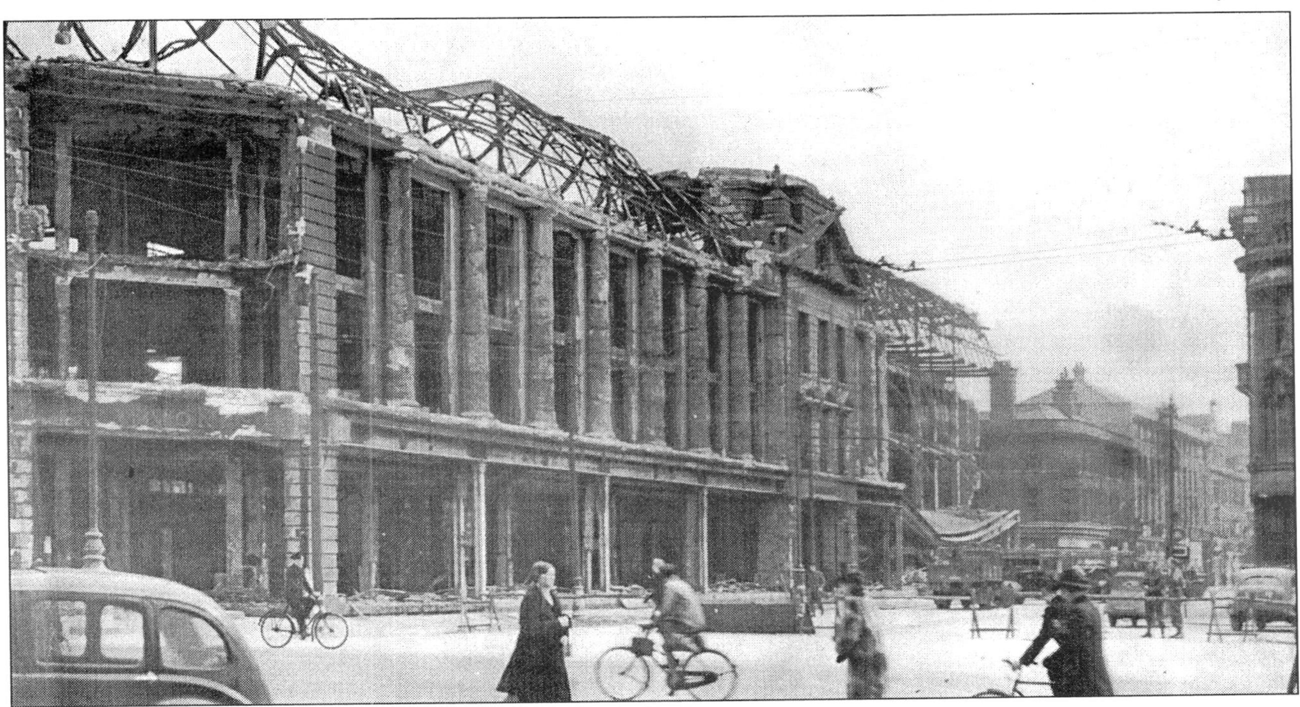

up papers. Hammond's staff who had been drafted into the forces, John Powell among them, were very conscious that things had changed and, though business in the store continued briskly, there were the first indications of problems which would become acute over the next 5½ years. The sale catalogue could not be issued in its usual format. Goods were difficult to obtain, deliveries uncertain and prices unstable. Samples of wool and material were normally distributed with the catalogue but, in the new climate of economy, this was considered wasteful. Hammond's would now only respond to specific requests. Owing to the emergency withdrawal of old contracts it was regretted that prices would have to be revised. There was, nevertheless, a wide selection of wool still available, though another response to the demands of war was an advertisement depicting surprisingly cheerful men in military and civil defence uniforms, listing the type of wool and needles recommended for knitting balaclava helmets, socks, scarves, mittens, gloves and, for an officer type, a cardigan: 'Wools required for the above garments will be executed at the lowest possible prices ruling at time of delivery.'

This was all very tame compared with what was to come. Armageddon arrived with the Blitz of 7 and 8 May 1941 when the city centre was ravaged. 'It was apparent to those in charge that a heavy raid was to be made on Hull,' wrote *The Yorkshire Post.* 'The intensity of the raid [on 7 May] rapidly developed. Soon the Infirmary [only a short distance from Hammond's] seemed to be the centre of an inferno. There was the continuous crash of bombs, the unceasing roar of the barrage, and the loud smashing of glass. The noise was deafening. Violent gusts of blast from bombs exploding in the immediate neighbourhood shattered windows and rushed along corridors. Flames from near-by burning buildings gave awesome illumination to the interior.'

People in villages and towns miles away saw the night sky as bright as daylight. Hull was burning. King Edward Street and Prospect Street became a mass of flames and Hammond's, Thornton Varley's and the Prudential building were just three local landmarks which went in an orgy of destruction. Hammond's, opened with such confidence in 1916, suffered almost total destruction on the first night of the Blitz, possibly through a high-explosive bomb and a number of supporting incendiary bombs. One surprising survival of the attack, showing the ferocity of the fire which engulfed the store, is a cash box discovered in a safe in the Valuation Office. Two coins have been welded by the heat to the inside of the box.

For Hammond's staff their first sight of the ruins was a traumatic experience. Miss Lilian Shearsmith, who had begun work there in 1935, arrived as usual by train from Beverley to find a large space where the store had been the day before. Too upset to do more, she caught the next train home and, with tears in her eyes, told her family that Hammond's was now just a pile of rubble. But, once the immediate shock wore off, she was back at work in the West Street building which had survived and where business was resumed with remarkable speed; the air raid shelter now served as a staff canteen.

The spirit of defiance, determination and united effort was never stronger than at that time of physical desolation. Within a week 47 departments were somehow re-housed in West Street, buyers and staff quickly sorting themselves out, staking their claims to a place in a utilitarian building whose interior was never intended to be seen by the customers, built themselves fixtures and fittings from any old timber they could salvage from the bombed site, miraculously obtained stock and so enabled Hammond's to open for business once again.

It was a time when people rallied round unselfishly. There were marvellous examples of support from the business community. Many suppliers sent new merchandise without being asked and the managers of Hull Savings Bank in George Street offered the use of their Board Room as an office. William and James Powell and senior colleagues immediately moved in.

The Lord Mayor, Alderman S. H. Smith, was full of admiration for the resilience of Hull business people, highlighting one example which can be identified through circumstantial details as referring to William Powell and Hammond's: 'He arrived in the morning to find the great monument to a life's industry reduced to ashes in a single night. He might reasonably have accepted the situation and gone into retirement. Instead, he set to work straight away – to start all over again. As soon as his plans were made, he wrote describing them to the National Chamber of Trade, of which he is an official. His letter was, I understand, sent on to the Prime Minister – and rightly so!'

The Yorkshire Post's Special Correspondent continued the story: 'I went into one new store, opened in a back street where the firm had some store rooms. This bare building has been transformed into busy, attractive departments, with make-shift counters and fittings. From this centre the new store has spread sideways along the block, taking in an old butcher's shop, an auctioneer's showroom, and a small warehouse. A wet fish shop and a public house, still doing business, have got themselves mixed up in the new lay-out.

' "The only department store with a pub on the premises, as you might say," commented a delivery man, unloading lino into the storerooms – formerly the firm's air raid shelters.

' "We took our jackets off and made the fittings and things ourselves," said my guide from the Outfitters' Department – and I myself saw one of the girls, at the wool counter, doing a little joinery in between serving customers. "A few days after the Blitz – which wiped out the whole of the old place and everything in it (we didn't save a pin or a button) – we were open for business again. The only trouble is – remembering my orders and returning for rolls of material which aren't there any more!"

'I saw the Boss, head of one of the North's biggest stores, seated in his hat, overcoat and muffler behind one of the counters and framed in a nice line of poplin ties, calmly busy with his correspondence.'

Later, a small part of the basement in the blitzed building was made water-tight and so a little extra space acquired for china, glass and ironmongery. The roof may have stopped rain but duckboards kept the feet of customers out of the water at ground level. At the same time as the main building was bombed, so too was the garage. By this time, though, much of Hammond's transport had been commandeered for war service. Those vehicles which remained were organised into a pool for deliveries and parked either in streets in Hessle or in one of the Hull parks.

From the temporary offices at Hull Savings Bank, William Powell regretfully informed Preference Shareholders on 19 August 1941 that the destruction of the store, shortage of goods, price regulations and rationing made it impossible to maintain the customary profits and pay the interim dividend due at that time. The current circumstances could never have been foreseen when the shares were issued in 1913. In addition he asked for agreement to a scheme for the reduction of Issued Preference Share Capital by 50%, a decision which would entail half their capital being returned to shareholders.

Praise for the way in which everyone made a superhuman effort to maintain business as usual in the most extraordinary times should not be allowed to obscure the profound sorrow felt at the destruction of a fine building and its beautiful contents, the product of so much work and imaginative planning over many years. Hull's colourful Stipendiary Magistrate, J. R.

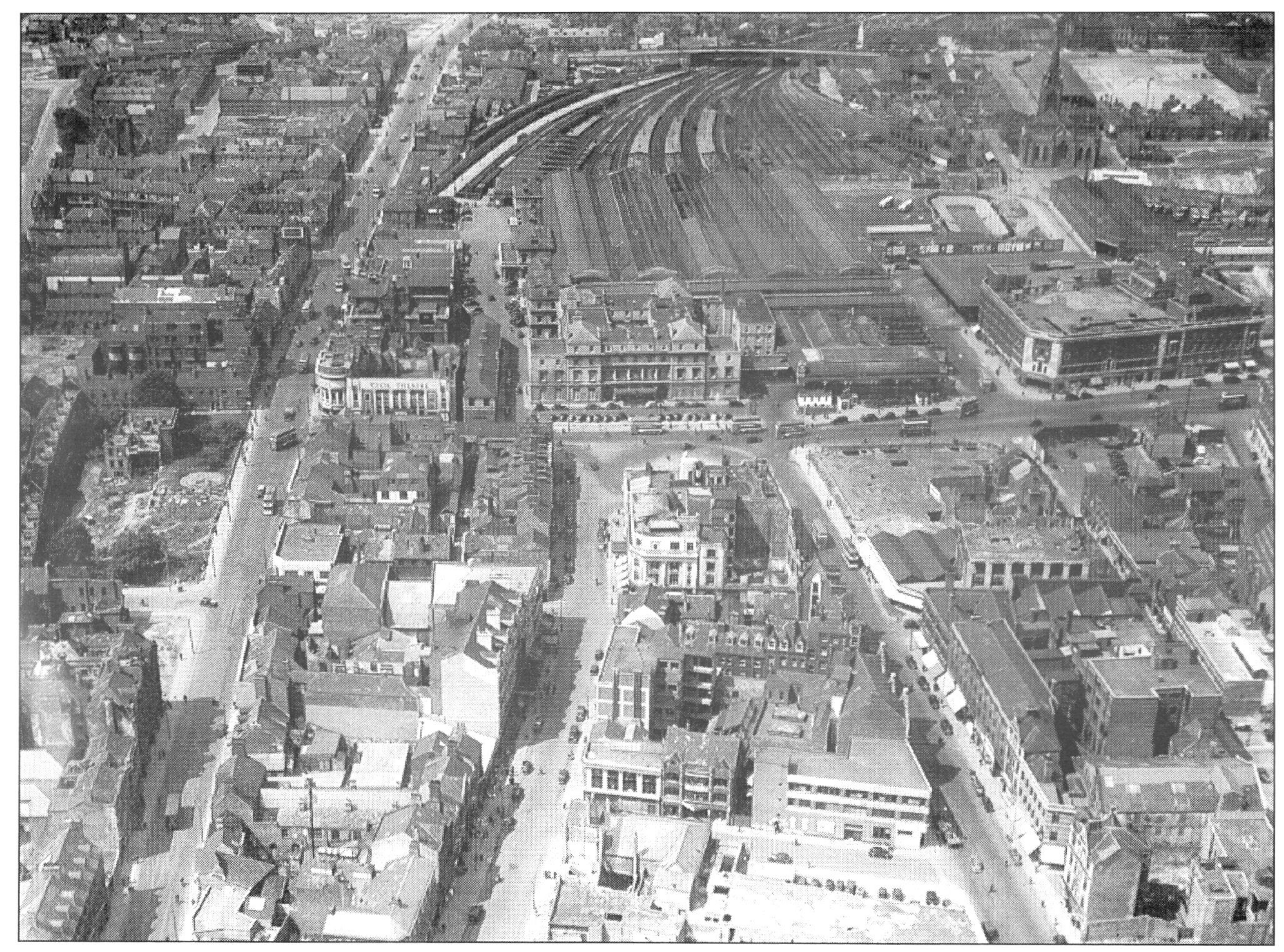

Aerial view showing the vacant site.

Macdonald, met William outside the ruined shop. He tried to convey his sympathy but William replied, 'Mr Macdonald, please don't talk about it. Fifty-two years of work and I don't suppose God will give me another fifty-two.'

The defiance shown in the aftermath of the bombing has been rightly and repeatedly lauded. On a much lower key but heroic in its own way was the quiet persistence needed to survive as the war dragged on; probably even more so in the years after the war which to many seemed the inexplicable and anticlimactic outcome of all their efforts. Stringent regulations governed the minutiae of trading. The use of company vehicles was limited by petrol rationing, utility goods were produced to strict specifications, prices were controlled by government orders and precise rules had to be followed on the number of coupons required for clothing. Any infringement of the law could lead to formidable penalties.

William Powell's melancholy musings on his own mortality in 1941 were fulfilled only two years later when he died in his eightieth year, outliving his two younger brothers, Henry and Samuel. For 35 years the head of the company, known affectionately to everyone as 'Father', he had been highly regarded in business circles. A devoted supporter of the drapery and allied trades' charity, the Purley School and Orphanage, for which he had raised hundreds of pounds, a prominent freemason and J.P. and founder member of Hull Golf Club, he had remained active even after the destruction of his life's work until a serious operation seven months before his death. Years later, his nephew, Christopher, received a letter from a Cottingham resident who had heard him give a talk on Hammond's. Her husband thought a great deal of William Powell: 'He used to tell me what a fatherly interest he took in all the staff, and I particularly remember being told how he could add up several columns of figures all at once in his head, what I always thought an absolutely staggering feat!'

It was the end of another chapter. The first two generations of Powells had gone, the third took over responsibility and prepared the fourth for their turn in due course. William's son, James, now became Chairman and Managing Director and, when victory

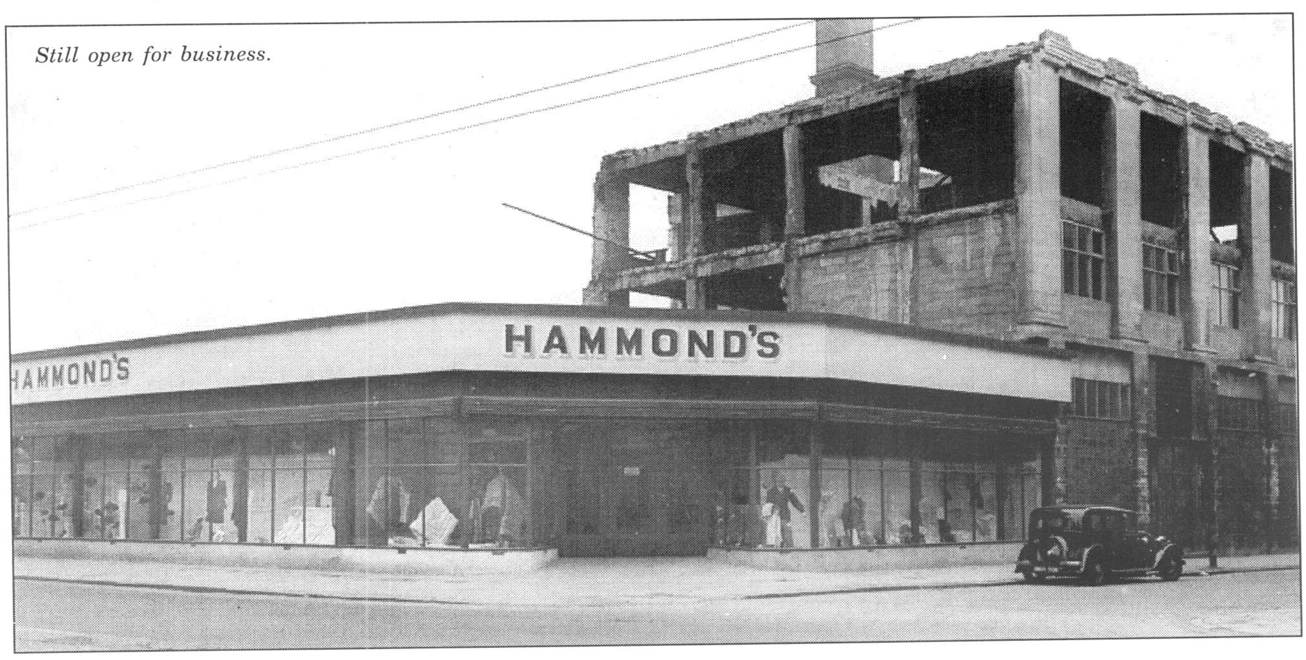

Still open for business.

finally came, the lucky ones, like his cousin, John, returned to pick up the pieces and steer Hammond's through a period when tenacity and hope were never more needed. A costly war had depleted Britain's financial resources. 'Export or Die' was the national mantra as the country struggled to balance its books. Goods for the home market were in short supply and many items still rationed.

Before Hammond's could replenish stocks, the coupons obtained from customers had to be sent to suppliers. It was time-consuming, frustrating and often depressing but some progress in improving accommodation was made in the years after the war in spite of the difficulty of obtaining licences for building or even for the smallest piece of wood. The old section of the basement still in use needed urgent attention. Usually it was two or three inches deep in water, and stalwart engineer Mr Alf Nicholson, who had already spent many hours re-building boilers and pumps, set about the job of pumping out all the water. Eventually it proved necessary to build a wall right across the site using underwater cement to hold back the water. Once this was completed, the space gained could be used for toys at Christmas and special displays of furniture, furnishing and wool.

After searching throughout the country Hammond's' directors eventually found – through what they admitted was 'rather a dubious source' – three wood and asbestos huts which had been erected just before the war in the grounds of an hotel in Minehead. These were purchased, taken down and delivered to Hull, and planning permission obtained along with the licence necessary for their re-erection. This basic accommodation was a great asset, providing space for Mr Archie Stewart's and Mr Dick Shepherd's departments. By some means Mr Edmund Thornton managed to produce carpet for the floor and, in those austere times when nothing was taken for granted, there was immense satisfaction that the result was 'quite a good fashion showroom'. Another – Nissen-type – hut was later acquired and erected at the rear of the showroom and used as a workroom and area for stock. It was not easy to provide even such a basic amenity as a staff canteen. Eventually Hammond's hired a wooden hut from the Corporation and erected it at the end of the West Street building on the site which later became the *Hull Daily Mail* car park.

Evidence of war lingered a long time. There was still an air raid shelter, but visionaries saw its possible peacetime transformation. Many difficulties had to be overcome to obtain permission to knock down all the internal reinforced concrete walls and convert the space for use by the china, glass and ironmongery departments and for a new shoe shop. In spite of the trauma of war and its aftermath, Hammond's put on a brave face to the public. Their speciality had always been wool and their reputation had been undamaged by disasters. 'For all your knitting and needlework requirements and everything for home sewing,' they reminded readers of St Mary's High School magazine that the obvious place to go was Hammond's Ltd. Wool Department in West Street. Tailoring services were also available, just as they had been in pre-war days: 'Ladies' coats and costumes, gents' suits and overcoats to measure. Own materials made up.'

One of Hull Corporation's attempts to help businesses was to build temporary shops in Ferensway. Hammond's saw an opportunity for themselves in this development and asked if it were possible to have a temporary building erected for their own use on the site later occupied by C & A Modes. This was agreed, they leased the site and the building became an important part of the business, housing their main furnishing departments, carpets, furniture and furnishing linen. An architectural peculiarity of this temporary building was that it surrounded a public house. A passageway leading from its front allowed customers in search for a drink to reach the front door of the pub. At the rear was another passage for delivery of beer.

While trading continued in the makeshift premises Sir Gordon Russell, the Director of the Council of Industrial Design, took the trouble to travel to Hull and open a small exhibition organised by Hammond's. Such special activities in the dreariest of times boosted the spirits of everyone in Hammond's and also, they believed, of the people of Hull.

Euphoria had greeted the end of the war in 1945 but a long, hard year passed before the official Victory Day celebration of 8 June 1946. It was no longer possible to suppress every complaint with the reminder, 'Don't you know there's a war on?', but the abnormal quickly became accepted as normal and, though there were many grumbles, most people were used to regarding problems and shortages as an unavoidable feature of everyday life. Staff bonuses had been resumed, and to mark Victory Day Hammond's directors gave each employee an additional payment of £2 – less income tax: 'It is felt that this will be a help to the members of the staff and in particular to the younger ones, enabling them to take a fuller part in the various forms of celebration which are being provided in the district.' It was, though, a staff much depleted from its pre-war heyday. From between 750 and 800, there were now only 330, a figure which included 60 returned ex-servicemen from the 150 or so who had been called up for military service.

7

The Battle to Rebuild

To local people it seemed obvious that, once the war finished, a new Hammond's would rise on the old site. It was, however, 1952 before this hope became a reality, and a decade of planning, campaigning against bureaucracy and endless determination to overcome obstacles was to precede the opening of the store. While the war was still at its height and victory far from certain, ideas for rebuilding were already stirring. By June 1942 James Powell was writing to T. P. Bennett & Co, architects, about 'plans for the future', although his main concern at the time was the state of the firm's bombed premises, not just in Paragon Square but also in Burden Street, West Street, Osborne Street and Myton Street.

Business was conducted by letter more than by telephone and urgent messages sent by telegram; fax and email were still to come. The result is the existence of thick files of correspondence, proof of the untiring stamina needed to bring any matter to a conclusion in that period when regulations controlled the most recondite areas of life. Sometimes laborious train journeys had to be made between Hull and London and rooms booked at Hull's Royal Station Hotel or at the Great Northern Hotel in London for face-to-face discussions.

The shattered remains of the Paragon Square store needed urgent attentions: the safety of the public, the possibility of flooding and the nuisance caused by smells and rats were major concerns. Demolition of what survived the inferno had left holes on the ground floor, with water seeping through into the basement. These holes had to be filled in and the stone staircase which had survived was taken down and rubble removed by horse-drawn transport and taken two miles away to Boothferry Road. On part of the site permission had been given for the Overseas Club to erect a hut for the duration of the war.

There were no easy solutions to many problems. The basement was deteriorating and much letter-writing was needed before licences authorising the necessary work were granted. Intensive discussions were conducted about the steel which had survived the fire: could it eventually be re-used or should it be removed by a government desperate for scrap metal? Even more contentious was the question of compensation. Two methods of calculation existed, the value of the property at the beginning of the war or the cost of re-building, which could obviously result in a much larger sum. Letters passed to and fro on the right way to proceed.

Early in 1944 the architects announced in the most general of terms that they had 'progressed in the matter of rebuilding Paragon Square' and produced their preliminary sketches on which they invited comments. James Powell made his views quite clear: 'the main elevation of the new building, whilst being kept simple in design, should, to people re-visiting Hull, be recognised as the Hammond's they previously knew'. This, he believed, could best be obtained by emphasising the corner and central entrance portions as the original building. Though the design changed, this principle was implemented in the building which eventually rose. One apparently small problem, yet requiring patience and diplomatic skill to resolve, was caused by a dilapidated, war-damaged – in fact, condemned – building, 59-63 West Street, which Hammond's wished to acquire and integrate in their property. The owner was well aware of the strength of her position and, when the time came, able to exact the highest price possible.

But far more fundamental was uncertainty over the future of the site itself. Would Hammond's ever be allowed to rebuild in the place they had occupied since 1916, one with outstanding advantages? Hull Corporation was using the massive destruction which had taken place as an opportunity to re-plan not merely the shopping centre but the entire city centre. Sir Patrick Abercrombie (originally in conjunction with Sir Edwin Lutyens) was working on a plan for a Hull of the future. There was no guarantee that Paragon Square would remain as it was and a cloud of uncertainty overhung discussions between Hammond's and their architects.

Ominously, on 6 July 1944, the City Engineer reported that the draft scheme for rebuilding Paragon Square had been postponed. Years were to be spent pressing the planning authority, at the least, to approve the proposals in principle and in objecting to the site's inclusion in any compulsory purchasing order. Hammond's offered to negotiate with the Corporation over part of the island site so that Ferensway could be widened. The issue, it seemed to the company, was simple. There were no complications over ownership of the site, the foundations were re-usable, no alternative site offered the same advantages and, whatever the layout adopted for a future shopping centre, it seemed obvious that it would be based on the continued existence of Jameson Street and – the comparatively new – Ferensway. The waiting game was to be protracted almost beyond endurance and it was 1950 before a positive decision was received.

Yet, in spite of frustration and continuing worries, the elevation of the new store was agreed, even complying with the demand that the name of the company should be displayed with the grammatical 'apostrophe s'. James Powell suggested that it might be advantageous to have a local architect appointed to assist T. P. Bennett & Co *in situ*. He first recommended Mr Alfred Blackmore of Blackmore and Sykes but soon gave preference to Llewellyn Kitchen of Gelder & Kitchen, the partnership responsible for the building since destroyed. His comment that Kitchen was conversant with 'the many difficulties that he had in connection with "rights of light" when building our old premises' is further support of his cousin John Powell's attribution of that design to Kitchen, though officially it is credited to the partnership.

The file of correspondence continued to grow and T. P. Bennett did not conceal his growing impatience with bureaucracy: 'The extremely dilatory way in which Town Planning schemes are being handled at present is a serious menace to rebuilding as few of our legislators seem to realise the long period of preparation that is necessary before an efficient building contract can start.' He hoped the Chamber of Commerce would continue to exert the utmost possible pressure upon Hull Corporation: 'Your own site at Paragon Square appears to be a site on which it should be a relatively simple matter to make a decision on building lines.'

But all could go wrong if sweeping recommendations in Abercrombie's much heralded and eagerly awaited report on the new Hull which would arise triumphantly from the ruins were to regard the traditional layout of the city with lofty disdain. The publication of the report intensified such fears. With considerable *sang froid* James Powell told T. P. Bennett that he had just heard something 'a little disturbing': if the Abercrombie Plan were adopted in its entirety 'our Paragon Square site will not be available for our own use'. With terrible irony it was proposed that Hammond's should be relocated to Osborne Street, which it had left for better things in 1916.

Abercrombie's vision did not, however, accord with that of many local people, who made vociferous protests. Their wish was to see the shopping centre rebuilt in its pre-war location, not moved to a site which would involve a long delay before normal trade could be resumed and serious technical problems in laying new foundations. In response Abercrombie agreed to prepare an alternative layout for a central shopping area and by 28 February 1945 T. P. Bennett was beginning 'to hope that we may be able to proceed with the plans for your new shop very shortly'.

Acquiring the old property, 59-63 West Street, became a more immediate issue when its owner died in May 1945. The heiress to the estate, her sister, made an offer to sell but, not surprisingly, at a price considerably more than the local estate agents considered it to be worth. In a letter to her solicitor she expressed her sorrow that Mr. Powell and his directors seemed 'determined to make negotiations so difficult in offering so low a figure as £8,000, and threatened to 'discuss the sale in another direction' if they did not come up with an improved figure. The outcome was inevitable, as everyone knew all along, the offer was upped to an impressive £10,800 and in July James Powell was relieved to report that, although the contract had not yet been signed, 'you may take it that we have acquired that bit of property in the centre of our main site'.

For Hammond's to be forced to retreat to Osborne Street, the shopping area designated in Abercrombie's first plan, would have been more than a case of déja vu. 'Most emphatically my firm does not approve of the proposed moving of the Shopping Centre to the Osborne Street district and would only consider going there if they were compelled to do so,' James Powell informed the Town Clerk on 29 March 1946 in a letter which made no attempt to conceal his indignation. Thirty-four years before, the public of Hull had subscribed a large part of the capital needed to make the move to Paragon Square, convinced that the site near the station had considerable advantages: 'I see no reason to think that this opinion has in any way changed. The shopping public were asking when they would once again make their purchases in "a decent shop" of the type they had enjoyed before the Blitz and [a thrust aimed at the conscience of a Labour council] old employees, many of them ex-servicemen, were asking, "When will you have accommodation so that we can have our old jobs back?"' The argument that Hammond's owned a lot of property in Osborne Street was vehemently refuted: all they had was a small garage in nearby Myton Street.

As a public relations exercise to gather support for their case, Hammond's published a picture of the store they envisaged occupying the old site. Underneath, the caption read: 'This is Hammond's as we would like to see it. It can only be done on our Paragon Square site. Please do all you can to help to get the shopping centre put back into its original position as soon as possible.' It showed a building reminiscent of what had been modern in the 1930s but rather a monolithic and monotonous design which never achieved reality.

Until the Council decided the building lines of Paragon Square a cloud of anxiety hung over the future, not least over the physical shape of the new store if Hammond's were allowed to rebuild. One plan drawn by T. P. Bennett shows the impact of the Planning Officer's proposals for the treatment of Ferensway and Paragon Square. A widened Ferensway would lead into a much enlarged Paragon Square, now crescent-shaped, with the Cenotaph as its focal point. Hammond's would be a substantially reduced L-shaped store, lacking its grand frontage towards Paragon Station and its advantageous corner site. Hammond's held out tenaciously for a rectangular building, citing in support of their argument the fact that a large part of the foundations, 'which are extremely expensive piles', remained in existence.

The years passed by. Post-war Britain may have been a time of far-reaching social reform, but on the surface it seemed depressing and dreary, what one poet called 'the sepia fifties', with little sign that things were getting better. Rationing became more stringent than during the war (and was to remain in force for years), evidence of war damage lay all around and morale was declining. An immense, concentrated effort had been made to secure victory and this seemed an unfair outcome. Bureaucracy, entrenched in the power it had rightly gained when government control was vital to survival, resulted in a complex interchange of paper involving Hammond's, their architect and legal adviser, Hull Corporation members and officials and, ultimately, the Minister of Town and Country Planning. To the City Engineer's bald announcement in January 1948 that consideration of their planning application for rebuilding had been postponed, Hammond's gave an angry riposte: notice of their intention to make an appeal to the Minister for his immediate determination of the matter. Their side of the argument was explained with confidence in the justice of their case. The store lost in the Blitz had been 'a distinguished feature of the city architecture', rebuilding was in the interest of the citizens of Hull and 'there can be no legitimate reason for depriving us of that site'.

In August 1948 James, John and William Powell (John's brother) and their lawyer Robert (later Sir Robert) Payne met councillors and senior officers of Hull Corporation, after which Mr. Payne summarised the proceedings. 'It appeared to be clear,' he wrote, 'the Corporation have not any clear idea of the development of Paragon Square.' The threat of a compulsory purchase order which had so long hung menacingly over Hammond's was still not lifted.

Events have proved that Hammond's' objections to the moving of the shopping centre to Osborne Street were not merely based on self-interest. James Powell was convinced that the area south of Osborne Street could not 'be popularised for retail shopping purposes'. Its death knell had sounded when the main entrance to Paragon Station was moved from Anlaby Road, one of the main reasons prompting Hammond's move. The heavy traffic on Carr Lane would be a barrier to such a scheme for transforming the area.

On 26 January 1949 T. P. Bennett made a formal

application to Hull Corporation for permission to develop the old site. When two months had passed and no yea or no received in reply, Hammond's then claimed their statutory right to appeal to the Minister of Town and Country Planning, Mr Lewis Silkin, for a public enquiry. The history of the firm and the cogency of their case were once again spelled out in an ever-mounting accumulation of documents.

The public confrontation between the two parties came with the appeal proceedings, which began on 10 August 1949 before Mr A. G. Shoosmith, an inspector of the Ministry of Town and Country Planning, with Mr C. N. Glidewell representing Hammond's and Town Clerk, Mr E. H. Bullock, the Corporation. Mr Glidewell's case was simple and clear. Refusal to give planning consent had already delayed rebuilding by 4½ years and, if one added the time needed for all the necessary preparatory work and for the actual construction, it would be seven years after the end of the war before the new store could be opened. 'Procrastination had not merely robbed his clients of time, but it had robbed the City of Hull of what had been its largest and one of its most modern departmental stores.'

For the Corporation, Alderman W. E. Body, chairman of Hull Town Planning Committee, stated that replanning Paragon Square was needed to relieve traffic congestion and – unnecessary advice on a principle which had always been foremost in the minds of Hammond's directors – the architectural treatment should be so imposing as to impress people arriving in Hull by train. He was followed by the Town Clerk, who spoke of the Corporation's anxiety to see Hammond's rebuild in the city and of the help they had been given over temporary accommodation. But Hammond's had to be seen in the context of future plans for the city centre, an argument that Mr Glidewell countered with the riposte that the continued absence of any such major development plan for central Hull was the crux of the matter: 'Were the citizens of Hull, who themselves bore the brunt and burden of these bombs, to go to their graves without anything in front of them except a series of paper plans, constantly changed, or were they in fact to have an opportunity of seeing, enjoying and using as part of their everyday lives building facilities to which they were accustomed? This putting off and putting off in pursuit of the ideal was in reality putting off in pursuit of the unattainable ideal.'

This appeal to a higher authority was a strategic move which produced the reaction expected: before the Minister gave his decision on the report of the enquiry, representatives of Hull City Council were invited to an informal meeting in London so that he could discuss with them the principal issue involved. The crucial encounter took place on 17 January 1950, an opportunity for Robert Payne, Hammond's solicitor, to emphasise how the efforts of the architect (now knighted as Sir Thomas Bennett) to discuss matters with the Corporation had been rebuffed. Privately he explained that the problem did not lie with Hull's officers but with the committee chairman whose attitude and 'very definite views' were an obstacle to progress.

The outcome was everything Hammond's could have wished for. Robert Payne's view was that the Corporation were 'most anxious about getting an adverse decision and they appear prepared to go to almost all lengths to avoid it'. An agreed solution between the two opposed parties was now a real possibility. There was a flurry of activity resulting in Hammond's offer to withdraw their appeal before the Minister considered his decision, subject to the Corporation's acceptance of a number of conditions, the principal one naturally being the acceptance of Sir Thomas Bennett's plan. Hammond's in turn agreed to sell the Corporation a strip of land on the Ferensway side of the site.

The Minister agreed and, at long last, the day arrived – 2 February 1950 – when Chairman James Powell could issue a statement announcing that agreement had been reached. Magnanimously, he made a point of highlighting the help and courteous cooperation of the Corporation officers, against whom there had never been any personal ill-feeling. The news was given great prominence in the *Hull Daily Mail* and the *Yorkshire Post.* One totally spontaneous letter from a woman who had been a customer for 23 years expressed the general delight: 'It gives me real pleasure and Hull will seem more like its old self.'

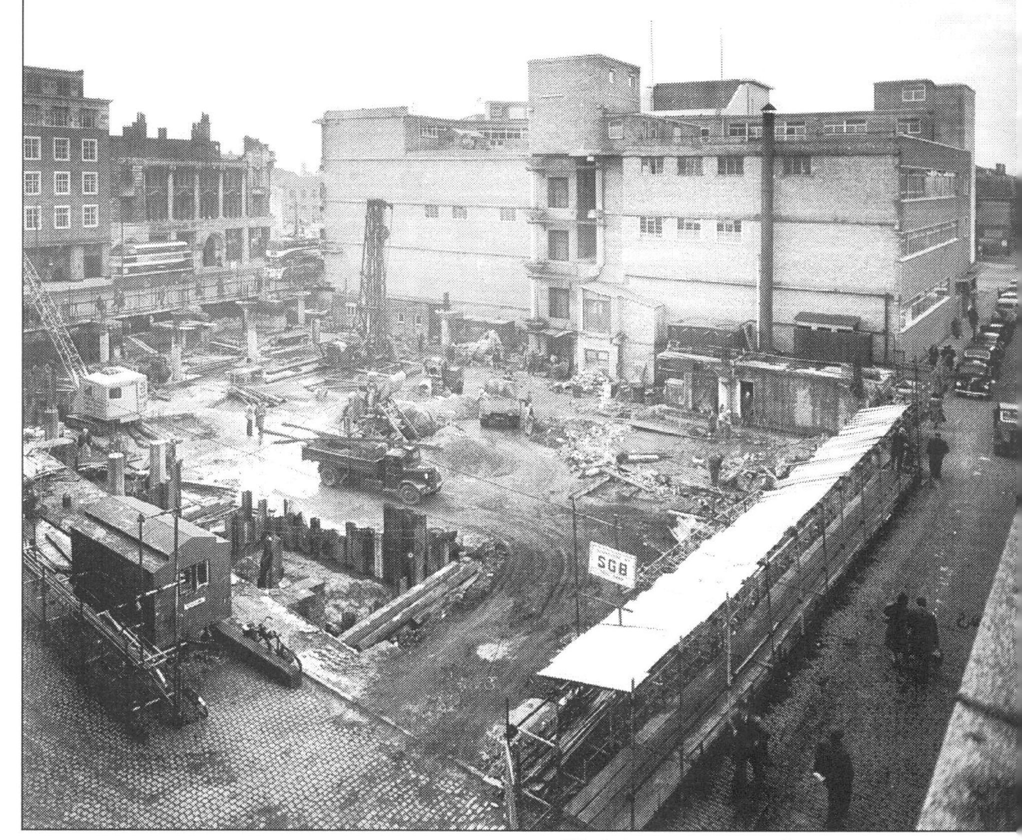

Work-in-progress on the new store.

In 1963, with the luxury of hindsight after more than a decade and with the new store in full swing, John Powell (Chairman since the death of James in 1957) could look back with a certain nostalgia and recall that 'to some extent we found fun in fighting after the war was over to re-establish ourselves and build a new store'. During the long years of frustration and delay the fun cannot have been very evident. Now that the go-ahead had been given, John Powell had to cope with an exceptionally heavy work-load. In addition to his normal duties connected with buying, selling and general administration, he had a multiple role as planner, builders' foreman and general dogsbody until the premises were ready for occupation.

Necessary demolition work was undertaken by Sam Allon (Hull) Ltd, the main building contractors were Sir Robert McAlpine & Sons Ltd, and one of the local firms involved was Toffolo and Son Ltd. Hammond's had agreed to set back the building 50 feet from Ferensway in order to comply with Town and Country Planning requirements, though compensation for this loss of space was the acquisition of the old property in West Street. Reinforced concrete was faced with Portland stone and glass-fronted towers emphasised the importance of the Ferensway and Jameson Street entrances. Hanging signs ensured that no one could be unaware that this was Hammond's. though a less stringent attitude to grammar now allowed the apostrophe in the name to be dropped.

Aerial view of the 1952 store

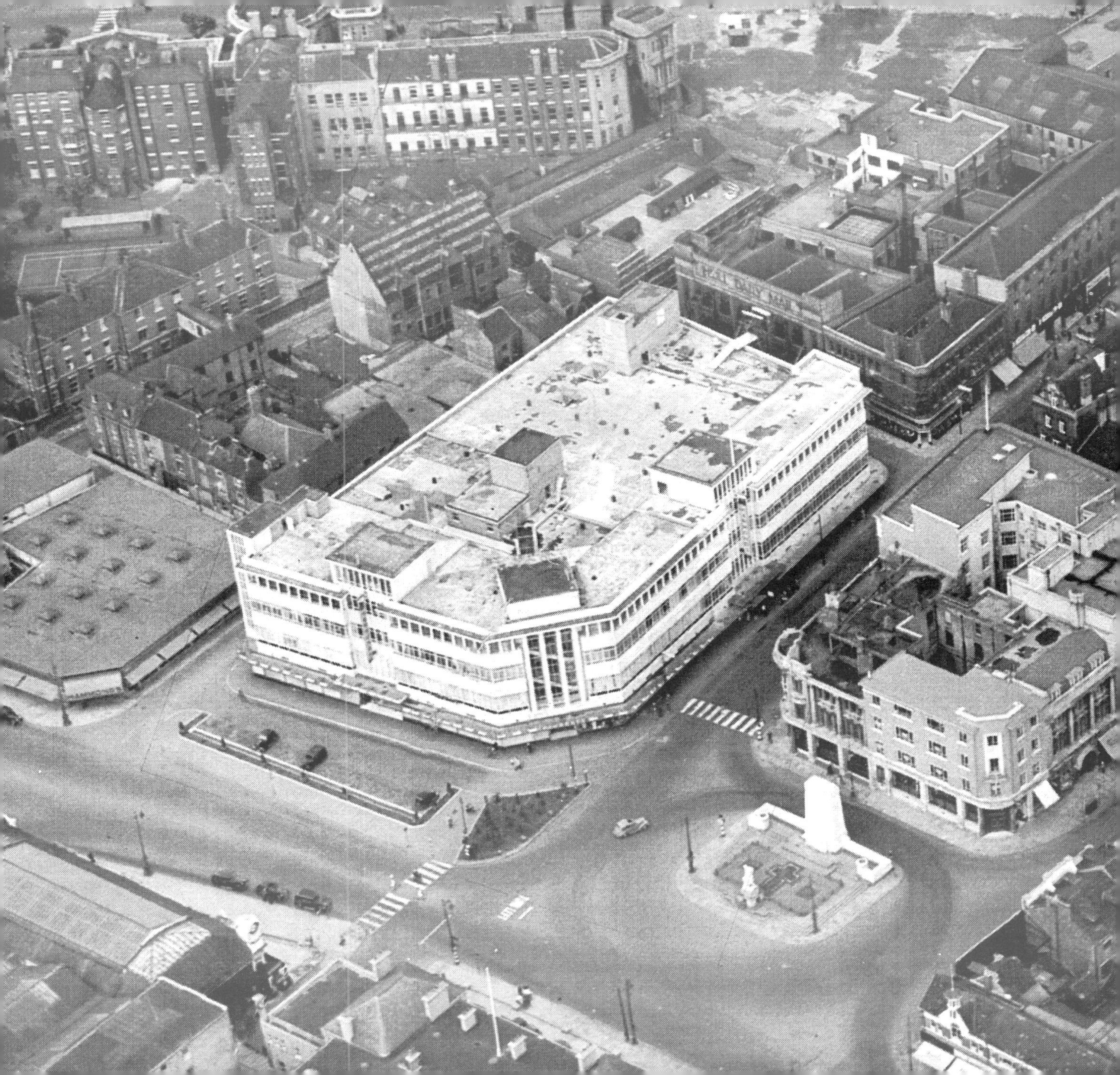

8

The New Store

The new store made an immediate visual impact on Hull's townscape. Its modernity was in dramatic contrast to what Hull had known before. Instead of the grandeur of the Edwardian Imperial style, previously thought appropriate for great business houses, and the timidity of neat but characterless architecture both pre- and post-war, Hull was startled by a gleaming white angular building designed on geometric principles lightened by huge, uninterrupted areas of glass.

For some it was too novel but one, perhaps unexpected, admirer was Professor A. G. Dickens, the distinguished historian of the University College (soon to become the University of Hull). Though he had a deep love of medieval architecture, he was critical of the mediocrity and lack of originality of the neo-Georgian blocks which had replaced much of what had been lost in central Hull.

Fixing a date for the opening of a building where work is still very much in progress was fraught with dangers, but the directors were anxious to open before Whitsuntide, 1952, in order to be ready to attract summer visitors to the city. No doubt there was relief that enough had been completed in time for the pre-selected day, though not as much as had been hoped. Only the basement, ground floor and first floor were ready. The second floor, which would house the restaurant, and the third floor were due to open later in the year. In the meantime the existing premises in Ferensway and West Street remained open. There was still a large hole (part of the old basement) directly in front of some of the Ferensway windows, the part taken over by the Corporation and not filled in, as promised, in time for the opening. Accordingly a bridge was fitted across it, near the main entrance. The pneumatic tube system was also not ready for use and, as a temporary measure, cash desks were put in place.

Friday, 16 May, 1952, was a day of celebration not merely for Hammonds but also for Hull. Enough progress had been made for the press to describe the scene in the most purple of prose: 'Rising like a phoenix from the ashes with a brilliant sun shining on concrete and glass'. It was a major step in Hull's recovery from the trauma and the aftermath of war, the first large department store to re-open with adequate premises.

To perform the official opening Hammonds had engaged Dick Bentley, 'famous stage and radio personality', a star of the immensely popular BBC comedy series, *Take It From Here*. The *Hull Daily Mail* described the lively scene: 'An hour before the official opening, crowds of women, gay in summer frocks, began to assemble outside the main entrance.

'The name 'Hammonds' was lit up in green neon lighting along the wide front of the building. On the roof the Union Jack stirred in a slight breeze, and men were perched on the edge, looking down on the throng.

'Along the front of the corner block, at first-floor level, gay garlands of flowers were bright in the sun. Across the wide entrance-doors, before the opening ceremony, a brilliant yellow ribbon barred the way to the locked doors.

'From points behind the transparent front, assistants in trim uniforms watched. Across the square, on the roof of the Royal Station Hotel, were maids in uniform.

'Men, women and children used the surroundings of the Cenotaph as a vantage point. There was an unbroken queue of women round from Jameson Street into West Street. Inside the building, 300 guests assembled for the opening ceremony, which was amplified to the big crowd outside.

'On the fringe of the great crowd, women held up small hand mirrors and compacts, hoping to get a "periscope" view of the opening. The heat was terrific, and one elderly woman had to be carried away.

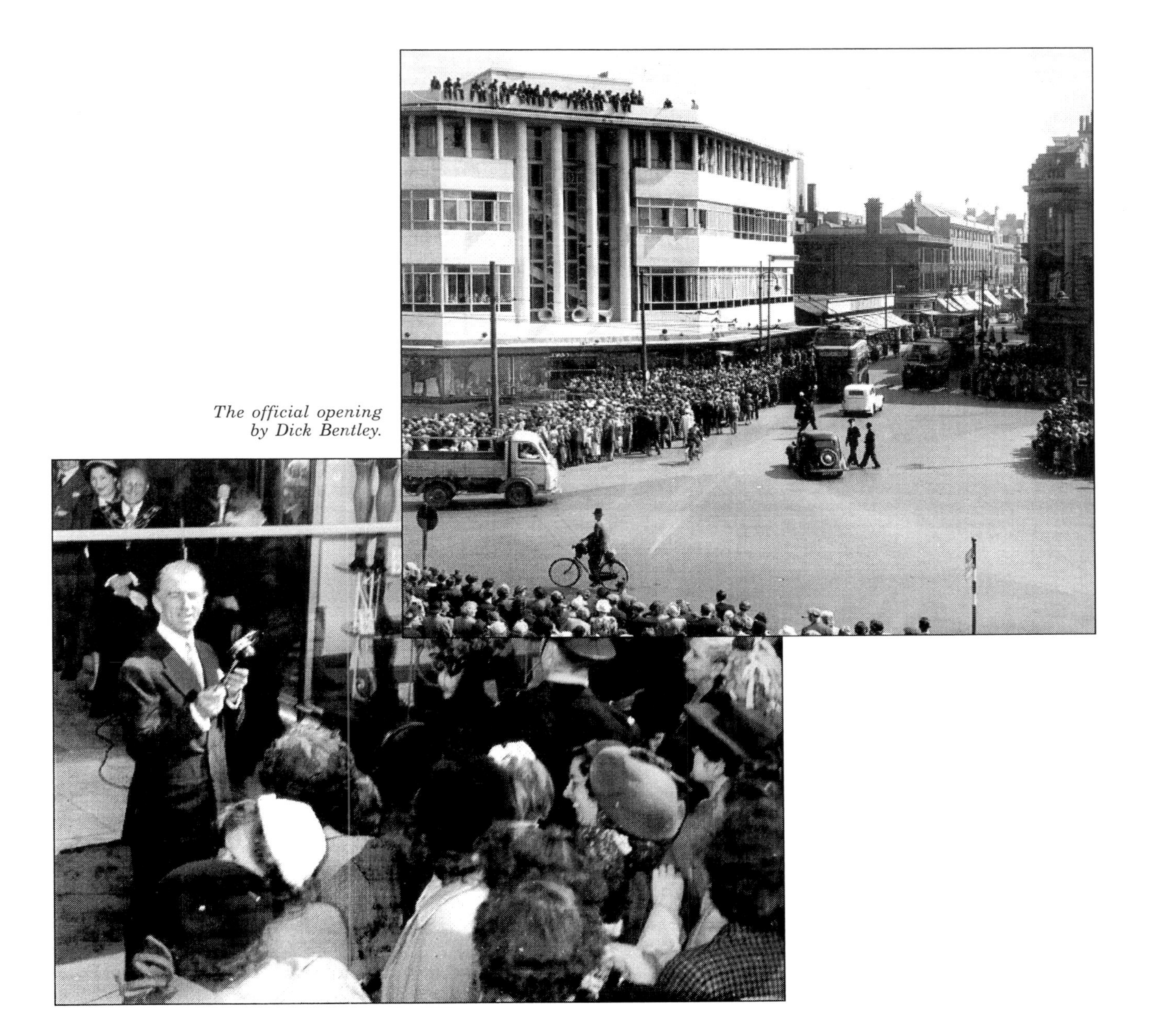

The official opening by Dick Bentley.

'Children cried in the crush and mounted policemen had continually to move the crowd back to enable trolleybuses to get through.

'One perspiring woman said, "I never expected anything like this." '

The firm's oldest employee, Jim Crawford, who had served Hammonds for 54 years, presented a bouquet to Mrs Bentley, James Powell recalled the long history of Hammonds and Lord Mayor, Alderman R. E. Smith, spoke of 'this beautiful new building', adding that it was gratifying to know that this was the first thing to be seen by visitors when they came out of the station. Over 300 guests assembled for the occasion and 200 enjoyed a buffet lunch in the temporary Nissen hut, which by then had been vacated by the Fashion Department. It was the building's swansong. That very same day, once the celebrations were over, Sam Allon's men arrived to pull it down.

Hammonds placed a full-page advertisement in the *Hull Daily Mail,* headed by a large sketch of the new premises, flanked on its left by a picture of the building it replaced, on its right by the Osborne Street premises and, below, the little Georgian shop near North Bridge.

An estimated 10,000 people thronged the area that day, no doubt attracted in part by the special offers and attractions Hammonds had arranged to bring in the crowds. These extra enticements included a guessing-the-cake-weight competition with a first prize of a holiday for two in Paris, a mannequin parade, a display of fashion through the ages, free gift vouchers in the Baby Linen and Children's Departments, a corset consulting service, an exhibition of furniture, a Hoover demonstration and, a sign of the times, a Television Corner: 'Daily transmissions of Television during the hours of BBC transmission [not then continuous throughout the day] when a large number of Receivers can be seen working side by side for your comparison in the comfort and privacy of our Television Corner.' Buying a television set was a major investment decision. Prices were far higher in relation to income than they have since become.

Work continued on the uncompleted part of the new building and departments were re-sited as more accommodation became available. When the central part of the third storey was ready for occupation in 1954, the toy department was moved from the ground floor and the space vacated was eagerly appropriated by other departments. So frequent were changes that the joke of the time was that, if you stood at the top of the escalator on a Monday morning, you would see three departments pass you.

All catering services had ended abruptly with the Blitz. After an eleven-year hiatus, Hammonds took particular pleasure in re-opening their restaurant. When the third floor was extended in 1957 (and an additional escalator installed) many people were introduced to a fairly new form of catering, the Picadish, a self-service restaurant, whose name won a television set for the customer who suggested it in a competition organised by the store. It rapidly proved a popular innovation for Hull at atime when eating places and pubs serving food were thin on the ground. This development particularly pleased Mr Clifford Verrando, the Catering Manager, who had been anxious to enlarge the catering facilities to reduce the length of the queues which were proof of the restaurant's success.

Austerity was still a recent, vivid memory but in the Picadish you were offered a tantalising selection of dishes, though still fairly traditional in style before television programmes on cooking and foreign travel had made much impact. Brown Windsor Soup (6d.), Heinz Tomato Soup (6d.), Rabbit and Bacon Pie (2s. 3d.), Creamed Tripe and Onions (2s.), Banana Custard (7d.) and Baked Jam Roll and Custard (7d.) and a long list of alternatives guaranteed the hearty, heavy lunch that was the custom before dieting took hold. A particular house flavour was provided by Hammondeggs (2s.) and Hammondburgers (1s. 3d.).

An upper floor was added to the building in West Street which had begun life as an air-raid shelter and provided accommodation for such behind-the-scenes facilities as the Staff Manager's office and staff cloakrooms. Another step into new territory came with the opening of a retail food department where you were tempted by mouth-watering displays to serve yourself. No one young enough to regard supermarkets as a normal part of the shopping scene can imagine the amazement of a customer entering a self-service grocery for the first time and, instead of standing at a counter and asking for goods with familiar names, being offered a wider choice than you ever knew existed and encouraged to cast economical housekeeping aside and experiment with items never appearing on a normal shopping list. It was modest by comparison with the endless aisles of modern supermarkets but it achieved its aim, opening up a whole new world of possibilities. The walk-round department store had helped to make shopping part of social life. Now, in a world which was growing noticeably richer, you were encouraged to make regular treats part of a sybaritic lifestyle.

Space was always at a premium and increasing business meant increasing pressure to expand, all made possible through a considerably increased turnover as optimism returned to the country, enabling Prime Minister Harold Macmillan to claim that most people had never had it so good. There was never a time when the programme of changes and improvements came to an end. The extension of the third floor in 1957 had allowed the Staff Canteen to be re-sited there as well as providing space for the Picadish. A dining room for the directors gave them a little more comfort as well as 'a little secluded place in which to argue'. In 1959 the hairdressing salon was opened there.

Even so, the Paragon Square complex could not accommodate everything needed by a growing business. In 1960 a warehouse was built in Spring Street to house the Food Group offices, packing rooms, Soft Furnishing and Carpet workrooms, as well as providing warehousing space. The top floor of the warehouse had a specially constructed roof to provide a large open space for the carpet workroom. Before the introduction of 'broadloom' carpets, lengths of 27-inch-wide carpeting were sewn together on a special machine and carpets were pre-shaped to fit the room before delivery. By 1964 the workroom could no longer cope with all the demands made on it and extensions and a new fourth floor were added, making Mr George Read, the man in charge, monarch of all he surveyed in Spring Street. Colleagues joked that from his eyrie he could now look enviously at Northern Dairies' headquarters, which he hoped to take over in the not too distant future.

Closer to the main site, the former Catholic school in Mill Street was acquired and passages built to connect it with Hammonds' existing property. At first-floor level a bridge linked the new fashion ticketing room and the fashion departments. But space was always at a premium: the bold solution to add a fourth floor to the main building to re-house offices, training rooms and the fashion workroom, so freeing more space for selling on the lower floors. An innovation (to which pre-war Hammonds had been opposed) was the introduction of internal shops, designated outlets for concessionaries, such as the Lotus shoe group, Dereta, Windsmoor, Eastex and Steiner. A Heel Bar was opened on the Lower Ground Floor.

Hammonds also took the radical decision to expand outside Hull. In November 1968 it was announced that Hammonds had bought two Bridlington stores, Carlton Ltd fronting King Street and Chapel Street, and Harry Davis and Co Ltd. Early in 1969 Carlton's was demolished and Stepney Contractors Ltd began work on a new building on the site designed on clean, modern lines by architects Elsworth, Sykes and Partners of Hull. One photograph taken at a historic stage of the construction shows John Powell standing on the roof at the 'topping out' ceremony. If his smile appears wan it was not through pessimism about the project but the outward and visible sign of his intense dislike of heights.

It was a significant step for Hammonds and a tremendous boost to Bridlington. Just as the press had once dubbed Bridlington 'Hull by the sea', so now they devised a headline 'Hammonds-on-Sea'. A massive advertising campaign extending to Scarborough, Driffield and Malton preceded the opening, culminating in one intended to raise excitement to its peak: 'We've been building up in Bridlington for Tomorrow,' it announced. 'Come and join us at 10.30 am for the opening ceremony.'

On opening day, 21 May 1970, Mr John Carlton first unveiled a plaque commemorating the site's connection with retailing since 1846 (the year the railway came to Bridlington) and occupied by Carlton Ltd 1918-69. Then, after a reception and luncheon for guests, came speeches by John Powell and the Mayor of Bridlington, Councillor F. T. Waterworth. 'We came to Bridlington with great expectations,' said John Powell. Nowadays, he explained, English resorts were suffering from competition from the sun and other Mediterranean resorts but Bridlington was a friendly place for people with families.'

The Mayor in turn was understandably delighted that Hammonds had given such a vote of confidence to Bridlington: 'If people like Hammonds can be influenced – if influence was needed – to come here it augurs well for the future for any others interested in the town.' Presentations followed: a key from Mr E. S. Barrett of Stepney Contractors to John Powell, and a bound copy of the site reports, 'Birth of a Store – a Year in Your Life' from Mr A. Johnson of Elsworth, Sykes and Partners to William Pearson Powell (John's nephew). Hundreds watched as the official party moved outside for the symbolic act of opening to be performed by John Powell's wife Brenda. To assist her in cutting the ribbon she asked the help of a six-year-old girl spectator, who was rewarded with the present of a doll almost as big as herself.

The new building, it was generally agreed, may have been modern in concept but it harmonised well with its older neighbours. It was the first Bridlington store to have an escalator and, with 30,000 feet of selling space, it employed well over 100 staff. An editorial in the *Bridlington Free Press* waxed lyrical on the consequences of the store for Bridlington: 'We must think and act in a progressive way. Taking our cue, as it were, from Hammonds, which, although spanking new and very impressive, is built on sound traditions and a legacy of local association.'

Tim Powell, director of the new venture, who had joined Hammonds in 1958,explained the reasoning which led to the expansion outside Hull. Bridlington was seen as a town of potential, the site was advantageous, and the store was near enough to operate with the same identity as the larger establishment in Hull but without the problems a normal branch store 30 miles away would have. Though obviously on a smaller scale, it offered similar services to those available in Hull and had one added advantage: a top-floor restaurant with a magnificent view over Bridlington, its beaches and the sea.

John Powell with his wife, Brenda, who cut the ribbon at the opening of the Bridlington store.

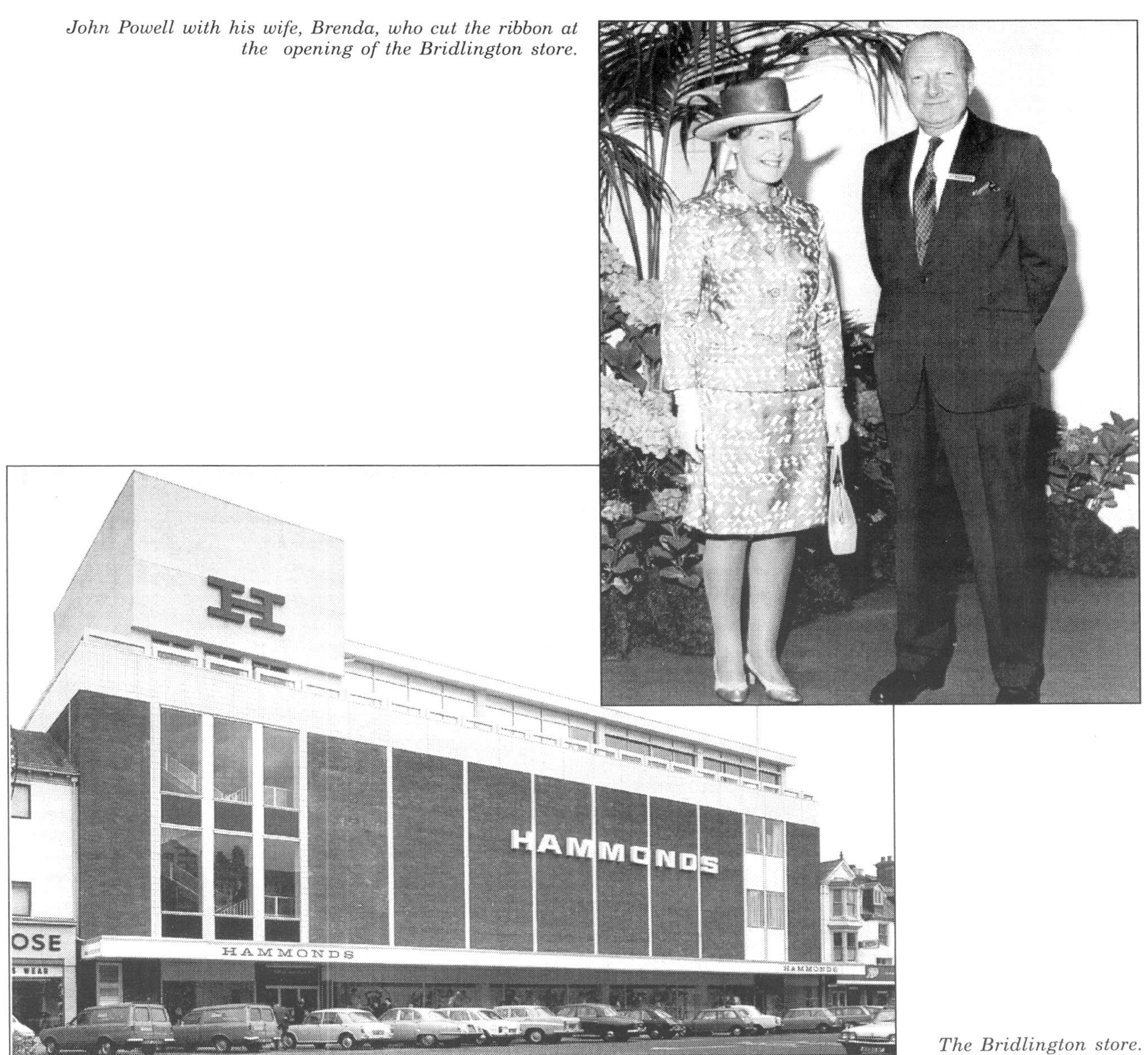

The Bridlington store.

9

Memories

So many former staff write and speak so nostalgically of their time at Hammonds that a historian of the firm risks being accused of sentimentalising the past. But happiness is a persistent theme of such recollections.

Mrs Neta Lowe, for example, was 22 years at the store and considered the china and glass department 'a delightful place to work', only retiring at the age of 67 after the take-over by House of Fraser, who required all women of 60 and over to leave, an issue on which the Powells ('really nice people') had been very relaxed. When Christopher, son of John, worked in the store during his college holidays, he would travel back to Hessle on the bus with herself and other Hammonds' staff and she would tease him about not riding in his father's car.

Christopher's own archive includes a typed statement of an amount owing to him after he had worked at the store during his school holidays. Dated 10 August 1953, and addressed to Master C. Powell, it reads, 'To one day's very hard work 10s with the compliments of Hammond's Ltd.' Christopher was later to train at Dickins and Jones, Regent Street, London and the well-known Midlands department store, Beattie's of Wolverhampton, before taking up employment in the store in 1961, the year in which his cousins, William Pearson Powell and Mark Patrick Severn Powell, had joined the business.

Those who worked for Hammonds considered themselves lucky to have found such a good employer. It could be a job for life and some staff built up impressive records of service, moving from Osborne Street to Paragon Square. A select few, surviving the Blitz and the straitened circumstances which followed, were still there when the new store opened in 1952. George Gee, a buyer who had worked for H. W. Hammond even before the Powells took over, had clocked up 60 years when he retired in 1948, too early to see the renaissance of the store. There were others who arrived at Osborne Street later than he had done and who spent their final years of employment in post-1952 Paragon Square. One employee, Matilda Dales, a showroom buyer, had a unique claim to fame. Though no official record survived of the exact date, it was known that she came with the founding father, James Powell, from Brighouse in 1889 and retired from Paragon Square in the 1930s.

To customers Hammonds was the smart store where everything functioned efficiently, cheerfully and – apparently – effortlessly. But, like a theatrical production, a whole army of – usually invisible – back-stage workers was needed to ensure a smooth production. One of those who worked behind the scenes was Tony Westoby, who emphasises the constant need for good maintenance in a large organisation under public scrutiny. That their efforts were taken for granted by customers (though never by the directors and managers) was itself a mark of their success.

For John Sanderson, maintenance electrician the years 1962-67 were the happiest days of his working life, 'I looked forward to going to work,' he says. There was a strong feeling of camaraderie and everyone cheerfully accepted the need to work out of hours when the store was closed. Hull was a great cycling city and each morning hundreds of bicycles were ridden down the slope into the underground park in West Street which had begun life as an air raid shelter. Mr Joe Heelas, the uniformed commissionaire, was like a regimental sergeant-major: 'If he said jump, you jumped!' Mr Heelas knew everyone and was much respected. His son, Peter, manned the Information Desk, where (before security became such an issue) customers could leave their shopping for later collection. Mrs. Katy King was like a housemother, looking after all the young

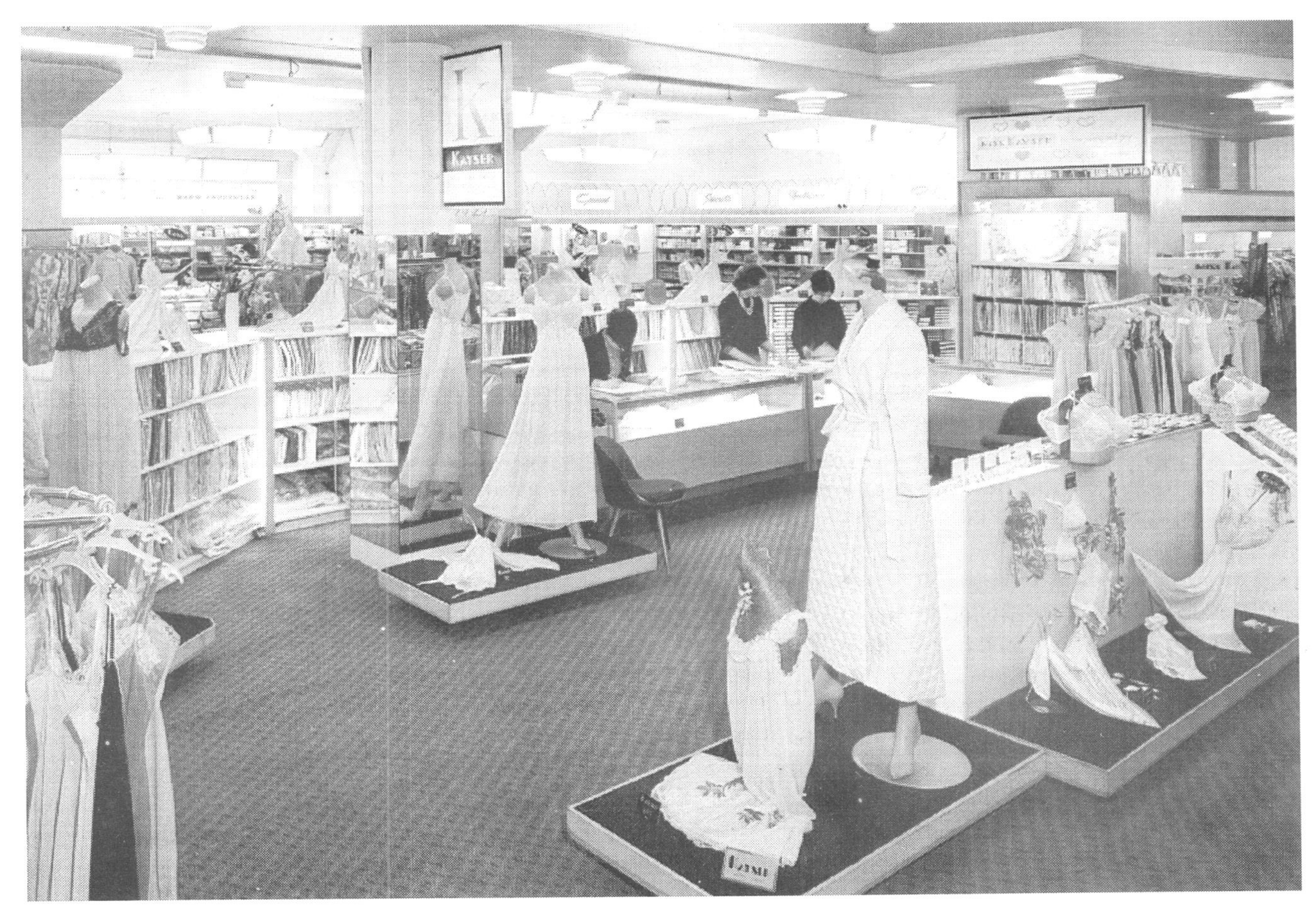

The spacious interior of the Hull store.

women on the staff, patrolling the store to see that everything was done right and issuing a 'friendly threat' to those who lingered too long over their lunch. John says that it was an open secret that certain 'posh ladies' would take dresses on approval, wear them at weekend functions and return them the following Monday as unsuitable.

There were many great personalities on the staff and Peter Heelas recalls some names which will stir the memories of those who worked at Hammonds during this period: Minnie Alden, Nellie Askew, Barbara Batty, Jim Crawford, Doris Firth, Teddy Hartell, Olive Kettlewell, Sydney Leeving, Jim Ryan and Bernard Watson. Others, not recorded, certainly made their mark in their day.

One of those who look back happily is Roger Gill.

He began as an apprentice upholsterer and feared for his future employment when he was injured in a serious accident when a bottle exploded. But Hammonds, in his own words, 'gave him hope when there was no hope'. A member of the Powell family told his parents, 'There will always be a job for Roger at Hammonds.' For a time he worked on the shop floor, collecting rubbish and doing odd jobs. Later he was put on the car park in West Street. His memories of fellow-employees and of customers are vivid, particularly of Peter Heelas and his father Joe, the commissionaire, who had previously had a similar post at the Tivoli Theatre. After 25 years Roger received the customary gold watch and after 35 years, less conventionally but at his own request, a lawnmower. He is eternally grateful to the Powells for the kindness they showed him when he needed it most. The tribute he pays could not be more sincere: 'We were a family.' Now a Hammonds' pensioner, he is still pleased to be kept in touch with what goes on and to receive a Christmas card signed by the directors.

Mrs Val Marsden (née Nicholson) says the period of approximately four years she spent at Hammonds in the 1960s as lift girl was the best job she ever had. She was particularly grateful to be employed by Hammonds as she had a heart problem which resulted in her becoming the youngest person ever to be fitted with a pacemaker. So happy was she in her work that she called all her passengers 'love' or 'dear', a style of address which Christopher Powell did not think quite right for Hammonds' customers. For a time she made a big effort with 'sir' and 'madam', but in the end she had to tell him that this formality was too much for her. She returned to 'love' and 'dear'.

It was essential to be smartly dressed. Her appearance was checked each morning to ensure she was wearing no flashy nylons and that her shoes were correct. For Val it was a real vocation. She looked after children while their parents shopped and kept sweets on a top shelf to make their repeated up and down journeys even more enjoyable. There were famous people who travelled with her, among them Jean Alexander, Margot Bryant and Pat Phoenix from *Coronation Street,* Helen Shapiro, Pauline Collins and John Alderton. Regular customers whom she learnt to recognise made her feel part of the family, and the Powells were always about. 'They never hid away in offices,' she says, 'and you could always go to them even though shyness always put me a bit on edge.' John Powell she saw as a very nice gentleman, but William (his nephew) was sterner and frightened her to death. She realised, however, that there was a gentleness beneath this harder exterior. Christopher was a 'smashing fellow' and helped her with fund-raising years after she had left.

Mrs Juanita Lewington (née La-Vigars) worked at Hammonds from 1951 to 1961, an interesting period of transition covering the final years of the post-Blitz 'temporary' arrangements and the excitement of the move into stylish modern premises. Progress on the new store was well under way when she started work in a little shop in West Street selling what were alliteratively if ambiguously described as Foreign Fancies: such frivolities as gifts, candles and artificial flowers. It was the first-ever outlet for Hornsea Pottery, though as it expanded its products were transferred to the China Department. A name like Juanita La-Vigars was too much for her first head of department, Miss Huby, to master and she decided to call her 'Vicky'; years later she is still Vicky to a few old friends. In those more formal days Miss Huby was always addressed as Miss Huby. Even now Mrs Lewington is unaware of her Christian name.

'Hammonds was a brilliant place to work,' she says. An unobtrusive but understood discipline underpinned everything that was done and the idea of service was a guiding principle. The atmosphere was friendly and positive, and, like other staff, she remembers that the

Powells were 'always visible', making everyone feel they were partners in a shared enterprise.

Staff parked their bicycles underground in West Street, where all goods were received, and Mrs Katy King of Personnel [the successor to the formidable Mrs Oliver] checked to see that hands and shoes were in fit condition for their owners to take up their duties. In the early days all females wore black dresses with white cuffs and collars; later, grey dresses were adopted as the house style. The first task each morning was to remove the covers placed over the counters at closing time. At the same time Joe Heelas, the long-serving doorman, took up his position outside, ready to open the doors to customers, who in the early days could park conveniently on a strip of land on the Ferensway side of the building.

The most amazing sight for Vicky was to see the queues waiting for the sales to begin and the mad rush to be first to the counters, some racing to the escalators to beat their rivals. Money whizzed back and forth through the chutes connecting counters and cashiers. Christmas was busy and cheerful. 'There was a real grotto then,' Vicky recalls, 'and Santa Claus was paraded through the city.' One year she dressed as an elf and became one of his little helpers. All the hard work was appreciated; a member of the Powell family, usually John, stood at the top of the stairs and thanked everyone for their efforts. A new social event, a departmental Christmas dinner and dance, was introduced by floor manager Norman Moss and later continued by George Watson. There were also parties for the children of staff. Christopher Powell recalls that the grottoes were prefabricated and assembled by the two house joiners, Mr Berry and Mr Lad: 'Berry and Lad, as they were known, were an unlikely team, Mr Berry being small, plump and quiet and Mr Lad tall, thin and full of fun. But they certainly made some magical grottoes.'

In summer staff were entertained by John Powell at his home Totleys, in Burstwick. It was an occasion when Vicky and her colleagues always wore their best bib and tucker – which included white gloves. The 'bonding' which is now so expensively and strenuously striven for on outward bound courses came more naturally and enjoyably through the Amateur Athletics Association and annual outings to a variety of places, among them the Lake District, Blackpool and Edinburgh.

Vicky was in the first batch of Hammonds' employees who studied for the City and Guilds Retailing Certificate on day-release classes at the College of Commerce in Brunswick Avenue. The course was very relevant to the students' employment, as it included visits to woollen mills and training in fitting shoes and corsets. She is eternally grateful for this opportunity which enabled her, after she left Hammonds in 1961, to pursue a successful business career in Canada, involving travel all over the world. Now returned to her native East Yorkshire, like all the Hammonds' staff who have contributed their memories, she looks back with great happiness: 'I thoroughly enjoyed my ten years there. They looked after us – it was a very good firm to work for.'

The Amateur Athletics Association, already referred to, catered for bowls, cricket, football, hockey, netball, small-bore rifle shooting, lawn tennis and table tennis. Most sections had teams in local leagues. The Association had the use of the British Railway Sports Ground in Chanterlands Avenue as well as the Social Club on Anlaby Road, where snooker and darts could be played. It also arranged dances and outings and held an annual garden party.

There were social events which did not fall into any of the recognised categories. Like Chris's Follies, which took the stage for a one-night-only stand in November 1961, when members of Hammonds Operatic Society entertained 240 members and guests at the Athletic

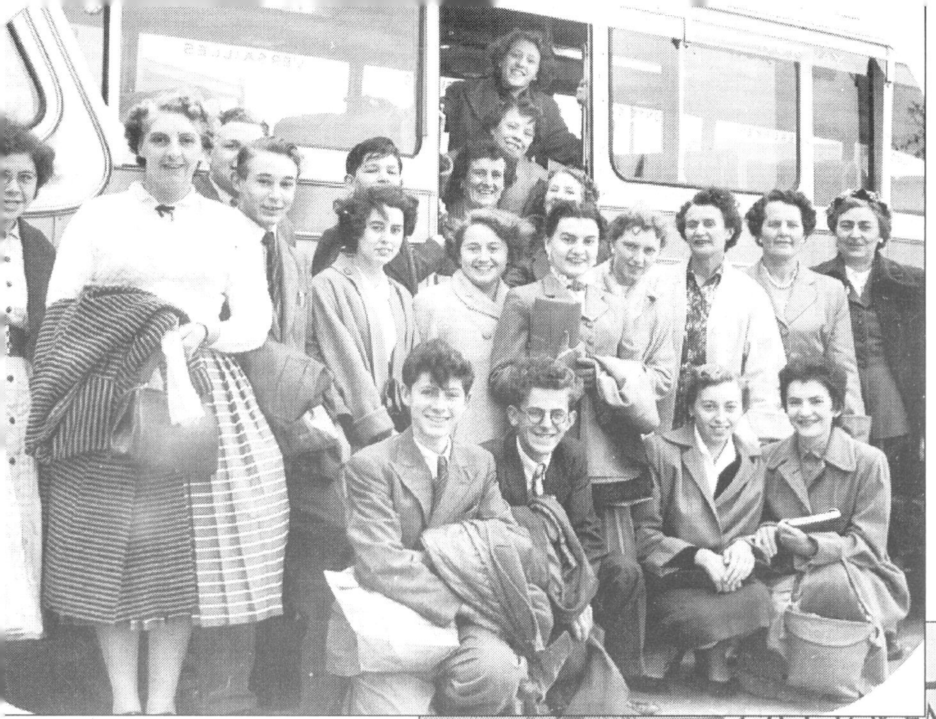

Association's annual dinner. Christopher Powell was the chairman of the drama society and the entertainment in which he took part was dubbed Chris's Follies by his cousin, William. The show may have had a limited run but it received impressive coverage in the *Hull Times.* One picture is of the eponymous Christopher in deer-stalker cap and cape, a wicked squire of the melodramatic school of acting, grinning fiendishly as he seduces a beautiful and patently innocent damsel.

Staff events – an outing.

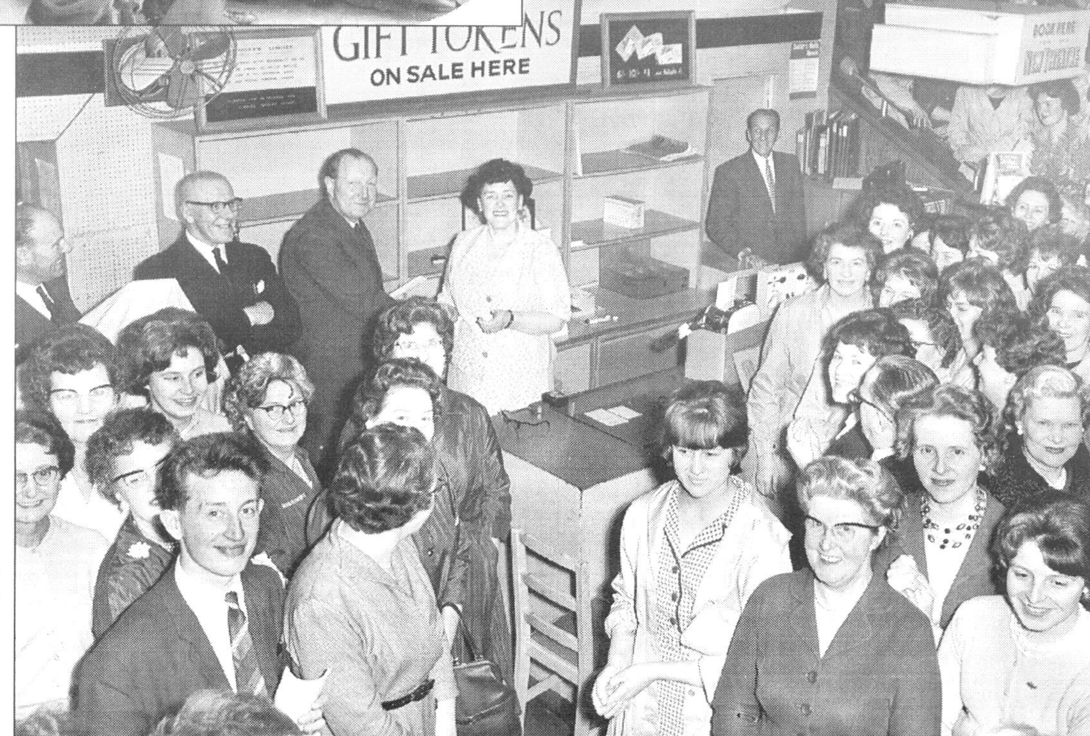

Another staff event — a presentation by John Powell.

10
The 1960s

In spite of the long-serving staff who never thought of leaving, the store employed such a large number of young women in their teens and early twenties that there was inevitably a fairly high turnover of personnel, particularly when marriage interrupted careers. The consequence was a heavy workload for the Staff Manager, Aidan Hughes, who was regularly occupied organising lectures, meetings and other events as part of a continuing training programme, one of whose aims, in a world of unstoppable change, was to help staff cope with the demands made on the retail trade by new designs, and new ideas on marketing. For some years Christopher Powell assisted him in the role of staff trainer. Together they attended schools' career evenings to promote the retail trade as a career.

Learning by watching an older person may once have been adequate, but the rapidity of change and the constant updating of systems made formal training programmes essential. As well as in-house courses, there were day-release schemes with fees paid by the company, attended by staff, like Juanita Lewington, at the College of Commerce or the College of Technology. Other courses were arranged with the Council of Industrial Design, manufacturers and trade associations. In addition to courses for sales staff, there were courses for other employees including office staff and those in the butchery department. Christopher Powell also instigated courses for senior staff to upgrade them on newer methods and introduced a Junior Management Course. It is a cause of gratification to him that all who attended this course have been successful in a range of other retail outlets, one even running her own shop.

Once the long-drawn-out tussle to have the new store built on the old site was over, business, in John Powell's words, became 'comparatively easy and we have been able to expand very substantially'. Yet a social revolution, almost imperceptible at first but with increasing momentum, was moving inexorably on. Traditional ways were being challenged and the lifestyle of many no longer conformed to the patterns carried over from pre-war into post-war days. More than ever, retailers had to respond to change.

The comment is often made that English people, unlike Americans and for reasons which have deep roots in history, seem, quite irrationally, to revere inherited wealth more than the achievement of those who acquired it by their own efforts in business and industry. Of all commercial activities selling has usually being regarded with the least respect. A major aim of the visits of Aidan Hughes and Christopher Powell to schools was to make parents and teachers realise that there was a career in retailing.

It was generally believed that the need to work on Saturdays was a deterrent to young people who might have embarked on a career in retailing at a time when the five-day week was becoming common elsewhere. To counteract this disincentive, discussions began, not only at Hammonds, on ways of achieving a similar objective by closing, obviously not on Saturdays but on another day in the week. The agreed, though not universally accepted, solution was to obtain a longer weekend for staff by closing on Mondays. Ironically, the future of retailing, in which supermarkets were an increasingly powerful force, was for much longer hours, which included opening on certain Sundays and on Bank Holidays, all of which would once have been unthinkable.

Thursday was Hull's traditional half-day closing, an innovation which had been welcomed by staff who worked the long hours once expected. But by the 1960s life had changed and many would-be shoppers regarded early closing on a busy weekday as a confounded nuisance. The passing of the Shops' Early Closing Day Act (1965) now gave traders freedom of choice and Hull City Council cancelled an old order concerning Thursday afternoon closure in the centre of the City, in force since 1913. Hammonds were prime movers in advocating closing the whole of Monday and remaining open all day Thursday when the subject was discussed by the Chamber of Trade in February 1964 but failed to secure enough support. However, a survey showed that a majority of customers favoured the change. From 13 September 1965 Hammonds would be closed all day Monday but, to compensate for the loss of trade, would remain open until 7.45 pm on Friday and 5.45 pm on Saturday. The more obvious choices would have been 8 pm and 6 pm but the selected times were handier for catching buses, which generally left at or just before the hour.

Other major stores adopted a similar policy – the result a curious melancholy atmosphere on a Monday in central Hull for those to whom it was still a normal working day and a relatively short-lived reform as people realised that what they supported in theory had practical drawbacks. Nevertheless, the results in the first year were very favourable, with increased turnover exceeding all expectations, so much so that at Christmas 1965 the Board decided to double the bonus previously paid as a mark of appreciation for the contribution made by staff.

The raising of the school leaving age to 16 and the introduction of pension schemes with a fixed retirement age meant there would be no more pleasantly emotional occasions when cheques were presented to those who had served Hammonds for 50 years. In these changed circumstances the directors decided to form the Over 25s Club, which all staff with 25 years' continuous service or 30 years' broken service would be eligible to join. At the time of its introduction there were already 27 candidates and a further three would join them within the year. For those who achieved 40 years an additional present would be given on retirement.

The reward, of course, was largely in honour and prestige but there were more tangible signs of recognition: in addition to the £25 cheque a silver gilded brooch for women and a silver lapel badge for men, these marks of distinction to be worn during peak trading periods, the first week of a sale, at special in-house events such as exhibitions, at company social events and at meetings of the club when new members were introduced. One member had, in fact, a double qualification. Miss Gertrude Colbourne had earlier been presented with a cheque for £50 for 50 years' service. She now became eligible to receive her emblem – but not, it was pointed out, a further £25.

At a ceremony (when lengths of service were not announced in order to avoid embarrassment to the female recipients) 'Mrs Sam', the widow of one of the three sons who had come from Brighouse, presented the cheques. For 58 years she had taken a very keen interest in the progress of the company and its staff and, according to the directors, had 'never been bashful or reticent in giving advice'. She had also been one of Hammonds' best customers.

On 24 October 1960 the 35 employees eligible for membership had accumulated an impressive total of 1,220 years' service. There were some notable recipients of the badges and cheques presented by Mrs John Powell and Mrs Marjorie Bradley, John Powell's director cousin. Among them were four brothers, Thomas, John, Eric and Henry Bootyman with an average service of 32 years, sons of the same Jim Bootyman, who completed an almost unbelievable 64 years with Hammonds. A husband and wife team, Mr and Mrs Len Harrison, had notched up 74 years' joint service, but the star of the evening was Miss Gertrude Colbourne, now with 51 years' service. After the presentations, William Powell unveiled a plaque on the third-floor staircase recording the founding of the club and the service given by members.

However attractive the covers, guide books issued to staff contain a list of rules and regulations which inevitably sound restrictive, even though in practice they are largely commonsense and not as formidable as they first appear. The ethos of the company emerges very strongly in the preamble to one such publication: 'Over many years Hammonds has earned the reputation of being a happy and friendly store; it is an attribute which, though having taken a long time to acquire, can be lost easily. Everyone is expected to set a high standard of courtesy, efficiency and helpfulness in dealing with customers. Of course, some of the non-selling staff do not have any direct contact with customers but all play their part in the growth of the Company and make it possible for the staff in the selling departments to be able to offer the standard of service and the friendly atmosphere for which the store is well known. All of us depend for our jobs upon the customers and the best way to ensure success is to **make the customers know that they can depend on us.'**

Things could go wrong, but complaints were to be transformed into opportunities to create goodwill. Staff should welcome and never resent such criticism:

'In dealing with complaints it is Hammonds' policy to give the customer satisfaction if possible and the Company is prepared to be over-generous rather than not generous enough.

'In settling complaints the Management will always support any action which favours the customer. It is important to remember, however, that adjustments made grudgingly after an argument do no good at all so in dealing with complaints always be pleasant, sympathetic and helpful right from the start.'

One reminder included was perhaps more necessary in later years when standards of dress in most walks of life were relaxed to an extent which would have appalled earlier shopkeepers: 'You must have a neat and businesslike appearance at all times.'

A career guide intended for prospective employees, particularly aimed at school leavers, struck a cheerful, positive note: 'To many customers the highlight of a trip to town means a visit to Hammonds for shopping, lunch in the restaurant and perhaps a new hairstyle.' Exceptional qualifications were needed by those who had direct contact with such customers: 'A sales assistant must have a lively intelligence, an interest in helping people, and an even temperament to be able to stand up to the hurly-burly of store life. The tempo of store life varies continually.'

Hammonds installed one of the earliest computers in Hull. It was supplied by National Cash Registers (NCR). Number 002 of that particular model which was housed in a specially built room that had air conditioning and heating. It was viewed by many with suspicion and rumour went round that it would do everyone out of a job, so the directors held a meeting of all the buyers and managers to explain what its role would be.

An NCR engineer spent many days and burned much midnight oil trying to get the thing to go. Geoffrey Knight explained that it was going to be used for preparing wages and then customer accounts. The Accounts Manager outlined how it would be introduced and a representative of NCR explained how it was being used in America. Question time. First question: 'Is it working?' Engineer said through his teeth: 'Not yet.' Whereupon the NCR representative stepped forward and said, 'You have number 002. Number 001 is installed in our head office, Baker Street, London, and if it is of any consolation that isn't working either!'

Staff were sent to NCR for training and were taught the emergency routine when there was a 'head crash'. This would be denoted by an alarm. The only problem was that NCR did not demonstrate the sound of the alarm so, when it did go off, it took the operator some time to realise what it was. She immediately followed the procedure but, in the time that it had taken her to react, 1.5 million characters had been wiped off the disc.

History, like newspapers, tends to focus more on events which are out of the ordinary than the unspectacular when people pursue a normal routine, taken for granted as long as it runs smoothly. No one, as far as is known, kept a diary of the everyday life of Hammonds' people, and the store may have been at its most successful when nothing made the news. One event which disturbed the even tenor of their ways was a serious outbreak of polio which spread alarm through Hull in 1961. John Powell, 'always well known for his philanthropic community spirit', as he was described in the *Drapery and Fashion Weekly,* turned Hammonds into an emergency clinic where lumps of sugar stained with anti-polio vaccine were distributed as part of a campaign instituted by local health officials. The ground-floor distribution centre was more convenient for many than the other clinics, and seekers after the magic sugar lumps, including staff and commercial travellers as well as the general public, descended in droves at the rate of 800 an hour, an achievement which was featured by both the BBC and Independent television.

Television has ensured that national and international events are brought close to home and, even if indirectly and subtly, they affect the moods and attitudes of people far from the centre of activity. At a managers' dinner in 1965 John Powell recalled recent events, the Olympic Games in Tokyo, the election of a new government, the death of Winston Churchill, and the exploration of space. 'Who knows, by 1970 or 1975 if we shall be selling tickets to the moon on the third floor,' he wondered, adding as a selling point, 'by Matador, of course', referring to the travel agents which had an outlet in Hammonds.

There were more immediate down-to-earth problems. Strangely as it now seems, remembering later problems of unemployment, there was difficulty in obtaining staff. Anxiety too had been stirred the previous year about the consequences of trading stamps, at that time a much-talked-about phenomenon in retailing. Since this initial concern the subject had receded a little into the background under the influence of Lord Sainsbury and his anti-stamp campaign, but it was still likely to re-emerge as another problem which would not go away.

Dr Beeching's planned closure of a number of local railways, in particular the lines to Withernsea and Hornsea, was causing heated debate and understandable anxiety over the horrors of life without the train. In the event it did not have the immediate, devastating impact foreseen by some. Through necessity both staff and customers quickly adapted to alternative road transport, either public or private.

About Hull City Council, John Powell spoke with wry humour: 'Our beloved Corporation tried their best with the one-way street experiments. Their race track down Jameson Street killed as many of our customers as possible before they could get through the doors. Luckily Mr Geoffrey Knight [administration and financial director] was able to persuade them that pedestrian crossings were necessary just in time. Otherwise we were considering putting the Medical Centre on the ground floor in some of the Perfumery Department's space.'

Parking was a problem which was destined to grow ever worse. It was the subject of constant discussion but there could be no final solution to the situation created by vastly increasing numbers of cars. A store situated near Paragon Station and handy for the bus station was still an asset but no longer the supreme advantage it had been when land was first purchased there.

Another of those unexpected and unwanted

happenings which disturbed routine occurred on Saturday, 24 October 1965. Suddenly fireworks exploded on the top floor. 'Within seconds,' reported the *Hull Daily Mail,* 'the department was like a battlefield, with choking smoke, the smell of burning and rockets and bangers going off. The department was packed with shoppers at the time.' Thousands of customers were evacuated from the packed store, among them women from the hairdressing salon, who escaped into the street with towels over wet hair and curlers. The firm's fire-fighting team went quickly into action, Hull Fire Brigade made a major turn-out and the police were soon on the spot. The fire, it was concluded, had been caused by fireworks let off deliberately, probably by three youths who had been hanging round the firework counter before making a quick get-away.

All the fireworks in the store were destroyed along with some toys and a number of radio and television sets, but normal business resumed elsewhere half an hour later. John Sanderson and his colleagues began work at 8 o'clock in the Saturday evening and continued through Sunday in order to have everything back to normal when the shop re-opened after the weekend. On the Monday morning he was putting the final touches to some pelmets when an early customer found him obstructing her progress. 'Why can't you work out of hours?' she asked. John, ever polite, did not reply.

A large store is a community and its history is told informally through the memories of its managers, staff and customers and in more tangible form, through the mass of papers, press cuttings and photographs, the archival detritus which remains after so much has been disposed of, lost or destroyed in war. Less gripping than anecdotes are directors' reports and accounts and the results of periodic departmental reviews. Yet the numbers and the statistics are the necessary thread running through the disparate parts of the story. The firm could only survive if it made a profit and, while the advertising campaigns, fashion displays, exhibitions and special promotions attracted all the attention they were intended to, a very close watch was kept on the objects at which they were directed: the number of customers, turnover, profits and year-by-year comparisons.

Such surveys were conducted with professional objectivity and Christopher Powell was given the same treatment as other managers with no suggestion of paternal favouritism. Comments from father to son range from the encouragement of 'A good start. Watch stocks', through criticism tempered with hope, 'Disappointing. Perhaps buying experience now gained will produce better results this year', on to straightforward praise, 'Very good turnover and profit'.

West 28 Street, a boutique selling fashionable menswear, caused continuing concern and in March 1968 John told Christopher, 'I must impress upon you the importance of watching stocks at West 28 Street'. A year later the problem remained: 'The results of West 28 Street do not meet the overhead costs of the shop. The Board did consider closing the shop down completely, but we have decided to give it one more year.'

Profits for the 1950s and 1960s indicate the bottom line of a successful business:

	£
1957	98,209
1958	94,458
1959	103,618
1960	132,816
1961	135,911
1962	129,249
1966	507,778
1967	520,996

Inflation complicates the interpretation of results announced in the Directors' Report and Accounts, but the figures available do, at least on the surface, indicate that Hammonds were more than keeping pace with such monetary trends.

What strikes a historian reading through the Powell papers is that ownership and management largely by one family through four generations never led to complacency or a self-satisfied readiness to rely on an inherited reputation and name. Instead, the utmost professionalism ruled. Members of the family gained their early experience working for other companies and new developments in all aspects of retailing – design, fashion, advertising, administration and so on – were closely monitored. Hammonds were aware that they operated not only in Yorkshire but also in a national and international context in which they had to keep abreast of change if they were to maintain their position and, even more, to make progress. The family image was a strength to staff but within the Powell family itself the need for the highest standard of business efficiency was never endangered by any concessions to their close relationship.

The advantage of the Paragon Square location could not be taken for granted. Concern was felt that, as circumstances changed, the impact of some signs on the building had been weakened. Only from an angle facing the main corner entrance did the building make the dominant impression which was wanted. From the Ravenscroft corner at the junction of Jameson Street and Prospect Street potential shoppers could read Thornton Varleys' sign, but not Hammonds'. Bladons, too, could draw people in their direction. The opening of Woolworths, accessible from West Street, gave Hammonds the opportunity to make its presence felt more noticeably at that side of the building. 'It would,' one presentation noted, 'be an error to presuppose that everyone knows where Hammonds is. We deal in summer with a changing "out of town" population travelling to and from holiday.' Strangers emerging from Paragon Station, it was urged, should be immediately confronted by an irresistible invitation: 'After passing Thornton Varleys' showcase in the station what do you see? A new sign saying Hammonds restaurant would make every railway traveller [who had experienced railway catering]forget all about Thornton Varleys. In addition the same new sign would serve us well in the inter months for the tea trade. After all, neither the Regal nor the Cecil are concealing their restaurant from the public.' Clear signs in a more distinctive colour were needed, and even the removal vans required attention. Painting 'Hammonds Garage' above their address rather than a plain 'Hammonds', would at least stop out-of-town visitors knocking at the garage doors to do their shopping.

A milestone was reached in the Powell story when John, grandson of the founder, who was both Chairman and Managing Director, announced that he intended to take a less active part in the running of the business. In April 1969 he resigned from the post of Managing Director which he had held for 25 years, though continuing as Chairman. The vacancy created was filled by the appointment of Joint Managing Directors, Geoffrey W. Knight and Geoffrey G. Wilson. Mr Knight had been with the company 17 years, 13 of those years on the Board. His former position as Company Secretary was filled by Colin Michael Davis, who continued as Chief Accountant.

John's brother, William Wilson Powell, remained Deputy Chairman and the family involvement in the firm was revitalised by the appointment of three members of the next generation of Powells as directors. Timothy James Powell, John's nephew, who had joined Hammonds in 1958 became director in charge of the Bridlington store, another nephew, Mark Powell, who had joined in 1961, became Fashion Group director, and John's son, Christopher Samuel, with Hammonds since 1961, became director of the household

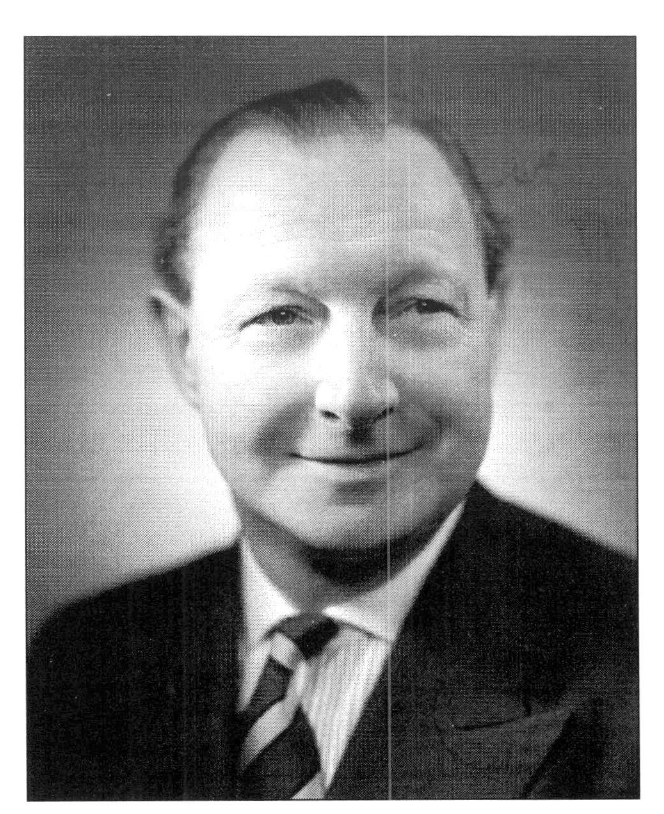

John Powell.

department with additional responsibility for public relations.

What became an unpleasant sign of the times, a hoax telephone call was received by the store's timekeeper just before 9 am on Friday, 27 June 1969. A male voice warned of six or eight sticks of gelignite on the second floor, where furniture, carpets and kitchen equipment were sold and where the restaurant was situated. It was the start of the busiest day of the week and over 1,000 staff and customers were immediately evacuated from the building. Once again the press photographed women with towels over their hair, expelled from the

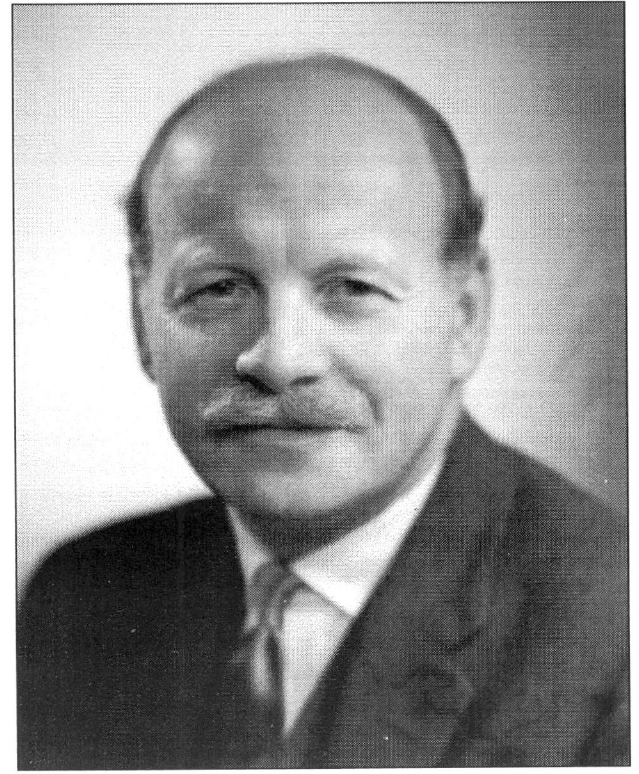

William Wilson Powell, John's brother.

hairdressing salon. However unlikely the danger, the message could not be ignored. There was just a possibility that a planned burglary had gone wrong. A thorough search was made of every drawer and cranny on the second floor, the entire building was probed and all waste paper examined before it was agreed that no cache of gelignite existed. After 75 minutes Hammonds returned to normal.

One letter received by the directors in July 1970 must have given them particular pleasure. Still treasured in the Powell family archive, it is beautifully handwritten, elegantly phrased and decorated with attractively coloured sketches by the couple who wrote it, Mr and Mrs Whitaker of Swanland Grove, Hull. Modestly they described themselves as senior citizens 'who have been fortunate enough to attain this rather advanced age and still be in possession of one or two faculties, which, as you will see, include slight artistic and literary tendencies'.

Their memories went back to 'those happy shopping days' in Osborne Street. Much in life had changed but they retained the same regard for Hammonds they had had in their youth. The quality of goods was reliable, there was never any cause for complaint and the assistants always seemed happy to be working there: a view shared by five generations of their family and their 'little group of discriminating friends in Hull'. It was a valued spontaneous tribute which fulfilled the Whitakers' hope that it would be 'a bit of a refreshing change from the vast amount of normal or humdrum correspondence arriving in your offices day by day in inconvenient quantity'.

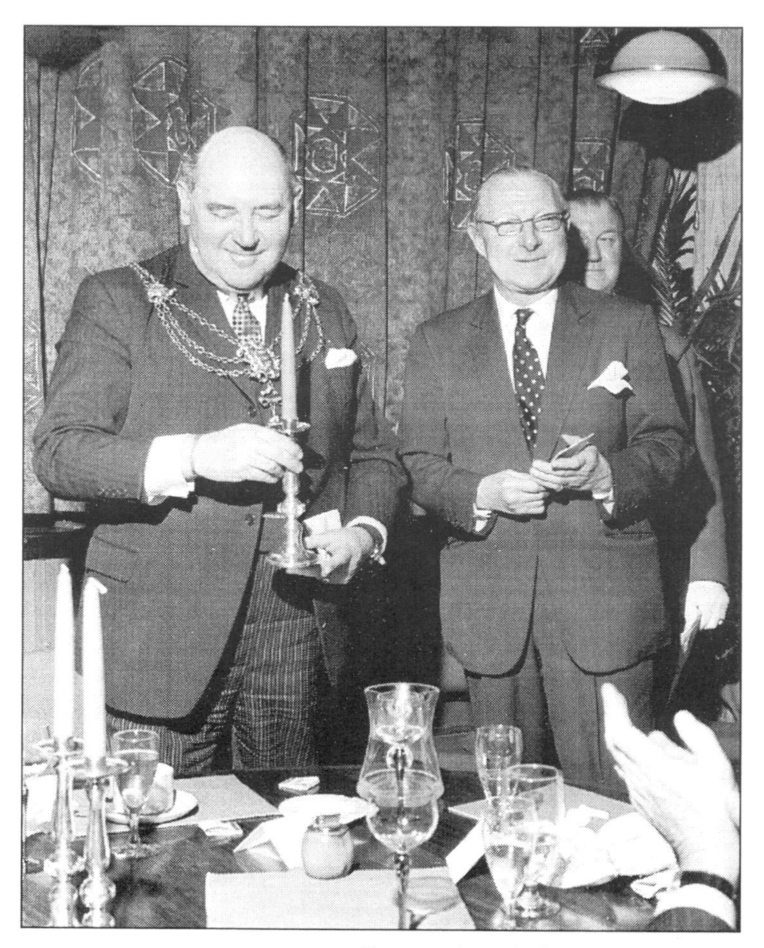

Presentation of silver candlesticks to Colonel Rupert Alec-Smith, Lord Mayor.

1821 hammonds 1971

Top to bottom, left to right James Powell 1889-1938, James William Powell 1889-1943, Henry Powell 1889-1923, Samuel Powell 1895-1933, James Powell 1919-1957, Marjorie Bradley 1941, John W. Powell 1931, William W. Powell 1945. Geoffrey W. Knight 1932, G. Geoffrey Wilson 1958, Timothy J. Powell 1958, William P. Powell 1961, Mark P. S. Powell 1961, Christopher S. Powell 1961.

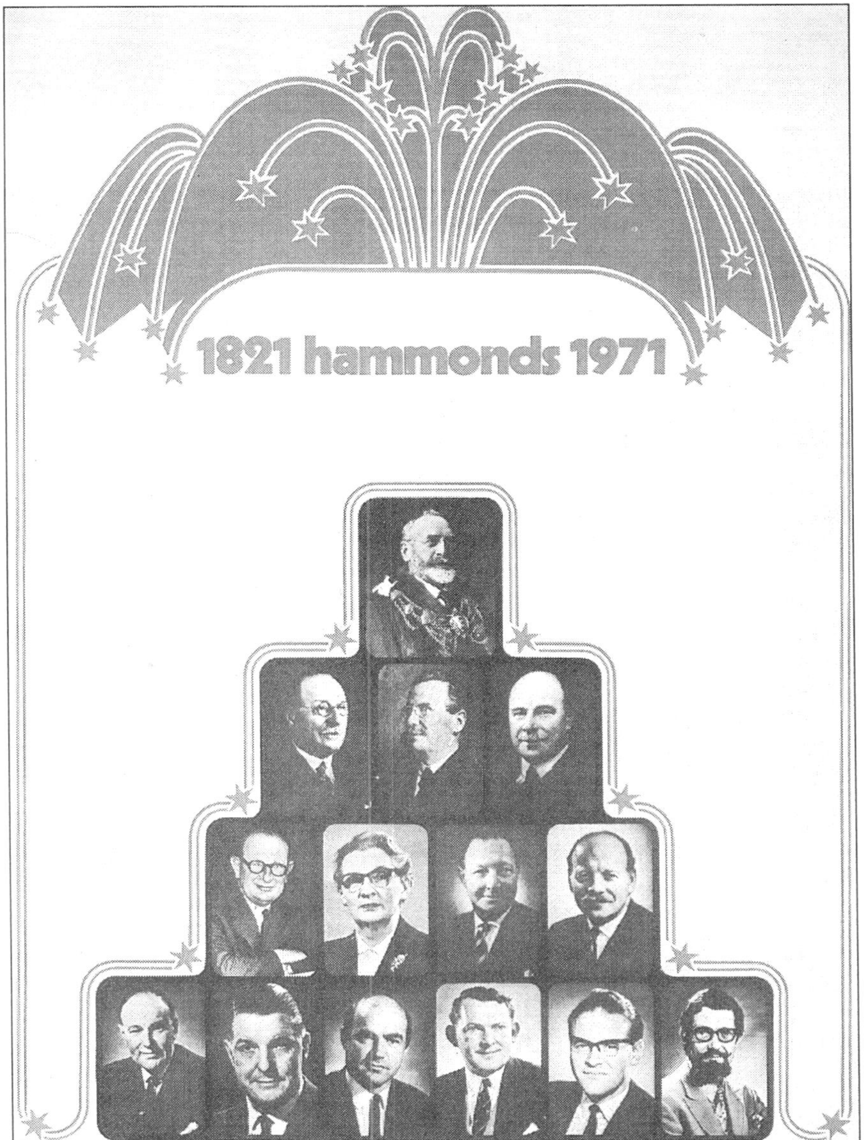

Souvenir of the 1971 celebrations.

11

1971: a year of celebration

The year 1921 had provided a reason for a centenary celebration with the added advantage of a splendid selling opportunity in difficult times. So, in 1971, the 150th anniversary of the accepted date of the founding of the store was a cause for even greater jubilation, an opportunity too for the erudite to air the extent of their vocabularies by making references to a sesquicentennial celebration. Advertising was extensive. A 16-page souvenir supplement published in the *Hull Daily Mail* told the history of the firm, accompanied by an illustrated 'family tree' of the Powells and of non-family directors, its theme the justifiable one of growth, progress and constant change for the better, and a clever pun, which nevertheless had to be pointed out to readers by inverted commas: of non-family directors. Hammonds was the 'buy-word' for Hull.

A catalogue of impressive statistics was produced. Hammonds employed more than 1,400 staff serving 7,145,500 customers a year – the then population of Hull 20 times over. On a busy day a check-out girl in the supermarket lifted four tons of groceries from basket to counter. Two hundred miles of dress fabric were sold annually, together with 10,000 pairs of footwear – and so on right down to 1,200 reams of tissue paper and 380,000 yards of adhesive tape. The gloomy days of post-war austerity were a thing of the past. Customers were enticed with well-designed goods, all in the latest fashions and all now theirs if they wished.

New concepts of design had been given much publicity by television and by the media generally. The subject attracted far more interest than it had ever done. It was, therefore, appropriate for Hammonds to draw customers in by a second-floor exhibition opened on 29 April 1971, '150 Years by Design'. There were five consecutive displays, each with a different theme, together forming the longest running retail promotion ever organised by the Council of Industrial Design.

The first display, of over 100 domestic items, was followed by 'Mainly for Men', 'Design on a Budget', 'Designers and their Work' (featuring two Hull-trained textile designers, Shirley Craven and Pat Albeck, as well as Patrick Rylands, John Clappison of Hornsea Pottery, whose designs were accepted by the Council for Industrial Design, Frederick Scott and David Carter), and 'Design for Tomorrow'. Special souvenirs commemorating the anniversary were designed by Pat Albeck and Hornsea Pottery. John Clappison's range of Hornsea Pottery specially made for the celebration featured Hammonds logo, the Big H. An accompanying exhibition told the history of Hammonds over 150 years.

Hammonds dressed their windows in accordance with the latest ideas and the Council of Industrial Design helped in the decoration of the store both inside and out. Other events included mannequins parading three times daily, in the evenings a series of lectures on design (one repeated in Bridlington), and a Beauty Fair ('a unique opportunity for the beauty conscious') supported by 14 leading cosmetic houses and, as an added inducement, not only free advice on offer but also 'lots of gifts given away with your purchases'.

One special event not open to the general public was a splendid reception, described by those who attended as 'truly regal', 'sumptuous', and 'an evening to remember', at which Hammonds entertained distinguished guests, business colleagues – and just friends.

Letters of thanks are always polite and often fulsome. But the words used in a thick file of such letters accumulated by John Powell show such a spontaneity and sincerity that no one can doubt that it was an outstanding event which demonstrated the high status Hammonds occupied in the local community and in the retail world.

An illustrious assembly was headed by the Lord Mayor, Colonel Rupert Alec-Smith, whom John Powell greatly admired ('in spite of the fact that I don't always agree with him'). To commemorate the link between Hammonds and Hull in a tangible way John Powell presented the Lord Mayor with six silver candlesticks to add to an already important collection of civic silver plate. Made to a modern design by Leslie Durbin, they bore the City's three crowns, the letter H for Hammonds, and the dates 1821-1971. Also present were the Sheriff, Basil Reckitt, a great friend of John; the Bishop of Hull; Sir Paul Reilly, Director of the Council of Industrial Design; and Anthony Heal of Heal's, London, Chairman of the Independent Stores Association. Many representatives of Hammonds suppliers, of local industry and business and the professions were present, among them, most appropriately, Mr Trippett, owner of a well-known surname, whom John Powell described as 'father of the retail trade in Hull'. He made special mention too of the *Hull Daily Mail,* with whom Hammonds had always had a special relationship and who had been extremely helpful in producing the celebratory supplement to that day's issue of the newspaper.

John Powell was presented with an illuminated address by Anthony Heal on behalf of the Independent Stores Association, but one guest, Max Zerny, of the long-established Hull cleaning firm, felt that there had been a major omission. 'The only thing that I regretted,' he wrote, 'was that no one amongst the speechmakers suggested that we all stand up and drink a toast to the Powell family and Hammonds. I know that most of us had kept a drop of champagne in our glasses ready for this.'

The anniversary served as a reminder to customers of their own long links with Hammonds. The granddaughter of Joseph Ostler was able to produce a shirt he had bought for his wedding in 1866 in the pre-Powell Osborne Street store, and Mrs Edwards of Hedon

Visit of Princess Margaret.

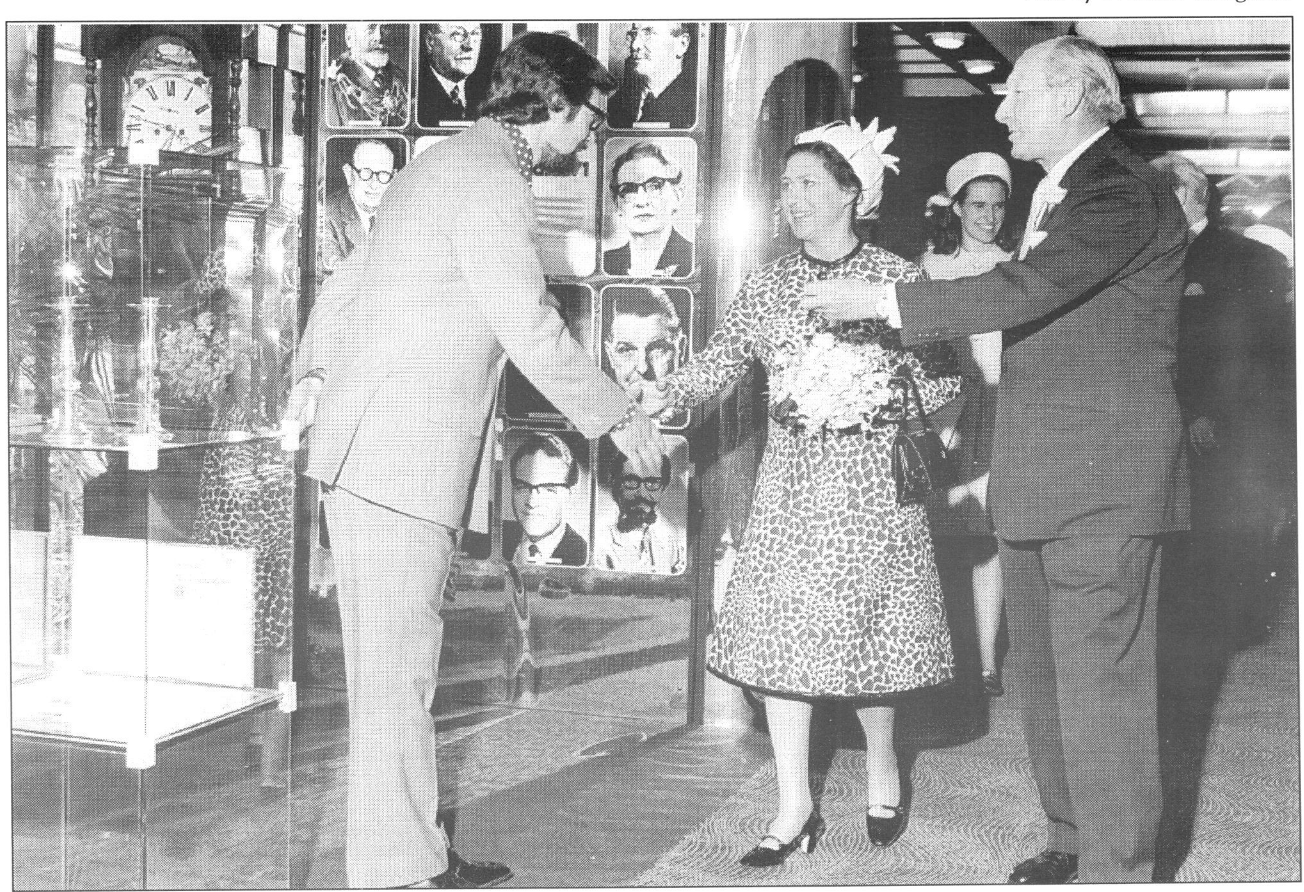

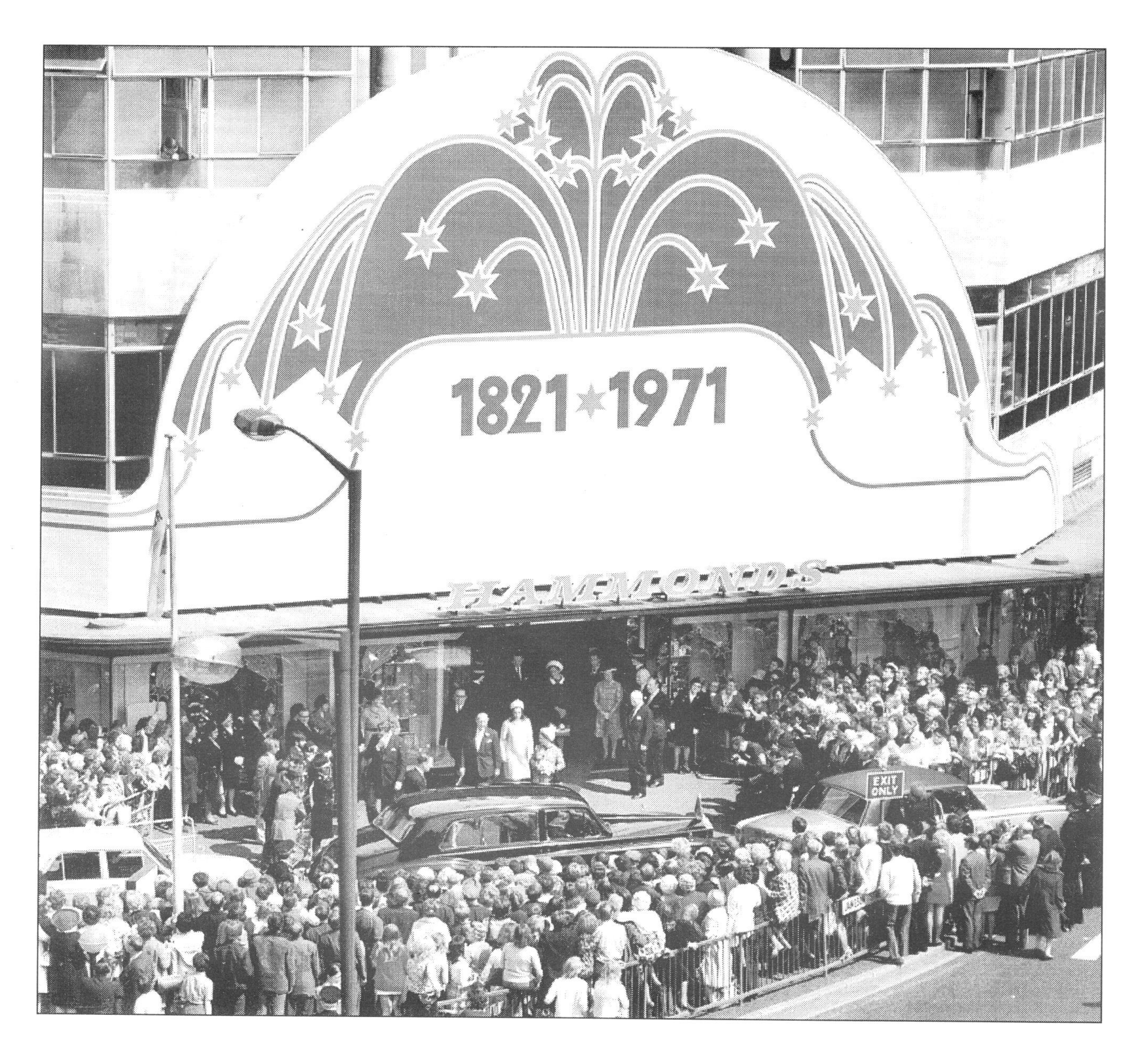
1821★1971
HAMMONDS
EXIT ONLY

sent John Powell an Osborne Street invoice for a sewing machine purchased in 1899 for £2. 16s. It was still in use.

An event, this time literally royal, came soon after, on 11 May, when Princess Margaret visited the store as part of her itinerary on an official visit to Hull. When she was shown the plaque on the staircase which had survived the Blitz and heard of Hammonds' speedy re-opening after its devastating loss, she remarked, 'That's the spirit that won the war.' Lord Halifax, the Lord Lieutenant, heard from the Palace that she had been delighted with the exhibition and with the enthusiasm of management and staff. One member of her entourage commented that it was the best organised visit to a store the Princess had ever made. Corroboration came from her detective, who told the Chief Constable that the visit was the best he had ever seen.

It was an anniversary deserving such an accolade – and all a far cry from the little drapery shop at North Bridge. Yet public euphoria could not be allowed to mask the continuing problems of running a business in a highly competitive market. One letter of thanks for the grand celebratory evening included a more serious note: 'I was very sorry to hear that you were having difficulty in improving net profit and return on capital and send my sympathies.'

Visit of Princess Margaret.

12

House of Fraser

The celebrations of 1971 were to be the climax of the Powell story. A year later, on 26 April 1972, came the shock announcement that, after negotiations lasting only two to three weeks, Hammonds was to be sold to the House of Fraser in a deal which they believed was in the long-term interests of shareholders, staff and customers. Geoffrey Knight, the Joint Managing Director, added to this explanation. The merger would forestall any estate duty problems which might arise with older shareholders as House of Fraser shares could be sold on the Stock Market whereas Hammonds (an unquoted company) could not. He also believed that the sale would give Hammonds better buying facilities as part of a large group, the House of Fraser being chosen 'because their stores are of a similar type to our own'. Hammonds' 1,250 employees had been assured that their positions would be safeguarded and there would be no change in pension arrangements for present or retired staff.

Sir Hugh Fraser, head of the huge international stores group, was equally optimistic about the future. Hammonds, he said, was already a very efficient business and the amalgamation could only make things better: 'All we wanted to do is to see that Hammonds goes from strength to strength.' Hull would benefit in future years from its key position in an area of growth, particularly when the Humber Bridge was opened: 'I am very much the new boy in the Hull situation and, although I am informed about possibilities for the future, the time is not yet right to say anything.'

On 8 May John Powell wrote to Ordinary Shareholders informing them of the agreed terms. Hammonds' net assets were valued at £4.2 million and the House of Fraser offer was worth approximately £8 million [in fact £7.9 million]. For each Hammonds' share House of Fraser offered shares worth £10.68, a sum 22.2 times the firm's prospective earnings. Already Hammonds' directors, who owned 64% of the total issued share capital, had given an 'irrevocable undertaking to accept the offer'. The next stage was to call an extraordinary meeting to increase the maximum number of Hammonds', directors (currently eight) to allow House of Fraser directors to join the Board. Although the terms seemed reasonable, even generous, at the time, increasing inflation after the sale meant that the deal was an excellent bargain for the House of Fraser.

The transfer of ownership took place in September 1972. However valid the reasons for the sale and however confident the forecasts for Hammonds' continuing prosperity, the news was received with sadness by staff, customers and people generally who felt that Hammonds was much more than a shop, a long-established local institution which they believed would always remain under local control. A significant break with the past was the retirement of John Powell as Chairman on 15 February 1973, the last of the family to occupy that office, and his replacement by Dr K. T. Morley. Five Powells, however, remained as directors.

A painful blow to local pride was House of Fraser's decision to change the name of the store to Binns. The new banner also went up on the Bridlington store. It was news which had a far greater emotional impact than ever expected by those who had considered it no more than a sensible name change which would incorporate Hammonds in the organisational structure of House of Fraser stores. 'Public response to the switch, which is costing hundreds of pounds, has been mixed,' noted the *Hull Daily Mail* with admirable restraint considering the way readers were bombarding it with letters of protest. Geoffrey Knight did his best to moderate the furore. 'There is bound to be some reaction against change,' he acknowledged, 'but the merchandise in the shops and the service will be just the same. The Binns group covers the North-East so it is fitting that we should belong to it and for administrative reasons it is better for the store to have the same name.' In spite of these soothing words, many older people refused to pronounce the dreaded word, Binns. Hammonds it had always been and Hammonds it would remain.

Though some members of the Powell family were still actively involved in the store, one casualty of the decision to change the name was Christopher Powell, who resigned as merchandise manager on 31 October 1973. It was, he said, the last straw and he completely agreed with the hundreds of people who had written to him denouncing it as a retrograde step: 'It had taken 150 years to build up the store to what it is, and there is still room for individuality in the High Street.' A former City councillor with strong ties with the arts in Hull, he was given a send-off at a colourful leaving party in the Arts Centre, Spring Street. He was leaving his post to breed quail, pheasants and guinea fowl in partnership with a friend on a farm in Holderness. Two Powell cousins, Tim (general manager in Bridlington) and Mark (general manager in Hull) were, however, to remain with the firm and keep the family name alive at Hammonds.

Public opinion can sometimes produce results. Hull people would never rest happy with Binns and the much-awaited day came in September 1989 when the *Hull Daily Mail* reported the wonderful news: 'Hammonds back by popular request'. 'There were huge cheers when we announced what we intended doing,' said Malcolm Scott, the store manager, 'and even louder cheers when we said it would happen.' Hammonds, he agreed, was a name synonymous with Hull: 'It was the essence of good shopping, good taste and had a kudos for the people. If, as I believe, a departmental store has a social role to play, it is important that the name relates to the city and the people.' The Hull store, he said, had become the jewel in the Binns group crown. Its large and pioneering food hall was one of the best outside London and problems which it experienced after its best year in 1981 had been overcome. 'In two years,' he explained, 'we have transformed the profitability of the store from being very poor to good.'

A £40,000 programme was started to change shop signs, stationery and delivery vans and, although the Bridlington store continued as Binns, on 20 September the old slogan could be revived: 'I could buy with my eyes shut at Hammonds and be sure of satisfaction.'

Inevitably in the post-Powell era, with the Hull store now part of a large group operating stores throughout England and Scotland, there was a greater turnover of managers than before. Equally inevitably, staff who had been at the store some time, like Geoff Ovington and John Sanderson, were very conscious of changes.

Yet there was no major alteration to the appearance of the building, still a landmark on its prominent site in

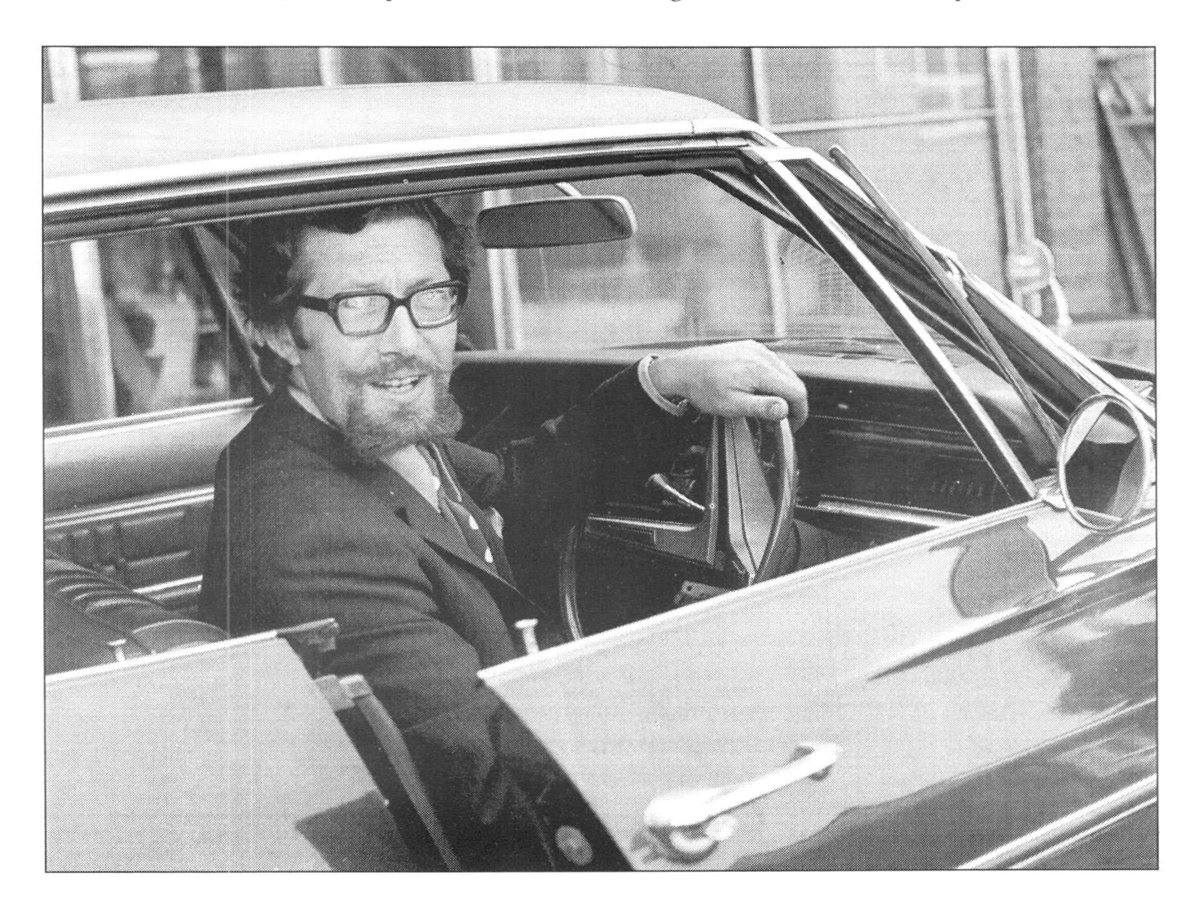

Christopher Powell.

Paragon Square. There was, of course, internal re-organisation over the next 30 years, as there had been from the earliest days, in response to changing needs.

In 1983 an additional coffee shop was opened on the ground floor and, more fundamentally, in March 1986 the Food Hall on the lower ground floor was closed as part of a policy of closure of Food Halls throughout the House of Fraser stores. At the same time the restaurants on the ground and second floor were closed and the third-floor Picadish was re-branded as the Bridge restaurant.

In 1989, the year in which the old name, Hammonds was restored, as it was part of a company now nationally managed, no longer on a regional basis, there was a major refurbishment; new escalators to all upper floors and new lifts were introduced.

Across in West Street the buildings comprising workshops and stockrooms along with the store's car park had been sold in the early 1980s and were subsequently demolished to form the NCP car park which later became part of the Prospect Centre.

In January 2003 the Spring Street warehouse, latterly used as a regional storage facility, was closed. It was sold to the developers of the Ferensway-St. Stephens project for demolition and to provide a site for residential accommodation.

Though now part of a large group, Hammonds still had a significant role to play. Through the 1980s it was the regional office for the Midlands region of the House of Fraser stores. During that time the store was a regional centre of excellence and was used as a training base for management and staff development and for the 'roll out' of new ranges and departments to the Midlands area. Since re-distribution of the regions in the late 1990s it has no longer served as a regional office, now forming part of the Northern group of stores which stretch from Edinburgh to Leamington Spa.

Hammonds is a name which evokes a list of associations. It needs no explanations: no one needs to ask what it is or where it is. Hammonds has weathered social change and war and its story is inextricably linked with that of Hull. Much more than a store, it is one of the City's great institutions.